The Sinners' Salvation

George Ryland

The Sinners' Salvation

Published by Ryland Books
P O Box 1461, Mulbarton, Johannesburg
rylandbooks10@gmail.com

ISBN 978-0-620-78265-4
eISBN 978-0-620-82156-8

2 4 6 8 10 9 7 5 3

All scripture references are taken from the
New King James Version of the Bible unless otherwise stated

Layout and cover design by Boutique Books
Printed by Digital Action

The following books are published under this Foundation series of books:

The Sinners Salvation Join a Church Baptism in Water

Baptism in the Holy Spirit. Study the Word Manner of Life

The New Covenant. Financial Blessings. Prayer

Soul Winning

Contents

Preface

I HAVE ALWAYS WANTED TO set in writing the things that God has taught me regarding the Word of God. I could see the great advantage that this would give believers who are interested in His Word.

Then, recently, in the light of a fresh new move of the Holy Spirit in my ministry, the Lord clearly directed me to set in writing the things that He has given me and He certainly gave me much to write about.

The fresh new move brought many new believers into the kingdom of God and these people needed a series of basic-concept principles. So I began to write and, as I wrote, so I learned and so I wrote and so I learned. I knew that this was the way to go and the Holy Spirit urged me to make haste and to write, because the work of God needed an injection of books that I had personally written.

I also realized that I had been in the ministry for more than thirty years, and that it was my responsibility to set pen to paper and to leave a clear record of my teachings, which I believe are founded in the Word. I pray that my books and other writings will add to the spiritual heritage that I hope to leave for my posterity, both natural and spiritual.

> ECCLESIASTES 12:9-11 ***And moreover, because the Preacher was wise, he still taught the people knowledge; yes, he pondered and sought out and set in order many proverbs. The Preacher sought to find acceptable words; and what was written was upright—words of truth. The words of the wise are like goads, and the words of scholars are like well-driven nails, given by one Shepherd.***

I pray that my writings will be in line with His Word and that many will be affected by His knowledge.

George John Ryland

Introduction

The absolute truth regarding salvation must be told. God expects me to tell, as best that I can, that which He Himself has revealed to the world. I do not have the right to water down, sugar coat or ease what I think might be too severe for my hearers. Neither do I have the right to only emphasize the good news of the Cross. If I am to be true to the Word of God, both sides of the coin must be clearly presented to lost and dying souls.

In this book I set forth the reality of Hades, sin, its consequences, the Judgement of God and Hell without any modification. The sincere would not be happy if I did not. On the other hand, some people would rather skip this part and jump right into the positive side.

Consider the following: if someone is fast asleep in a house that is on fire, would that person be happy if I walked by and left him or her in mortal danger? Must I not raise the alarm? I think that I must.

Readers will only grasp the beauty and the splendour of the cross, and God's plan of salvation, if they see, with absolute clarity, the horror that lies ahead for the sinner and also the wonder of His grace.

> ROMANS 11:22 ***Therefore consider the goodness and severity of God: on those who fell, severity; but toward you, goodness, if you continue in His goodness. Otherwise you also will be cut off.***

I must also set forth the wonderful and glorious grace of God that He demonstrated through His Son, without minimizing at all. Nobody would be pleased if I added or subtracted from it. What if I said that some good works were necessary to be added to the work of Christ? Would that be acceptable? Would that not prove that the work of Christ was imperfect?

If I found someone dying of thirst in the desert and I just walked by, although I had sufficient water to give him or her, would that not be cruel beyond measure? Must I not administer to life if it is within my power to do so? I think that I must.

Nobody who clearly sees that there is no need for any sinner to perish in Hell will plunge headlong into destruction, regardless.

Every sinner should read this book and should not rest until they have settled the matter of their salvation. If the clearly set out guidance that is given is followed, the sinner will be safely in the kingdom of God within the hour and earth will be the only hell that they will ever know. Earth is the only heaven a sinner will ever know.

All believers should also read this book so that they can be grounded in the knowledge of God's eternal Word.

George John Ryland

CHAPTER ONE

Hades and Hell

Whenever a person dies in his or her sins, they are immediately sucked down into Hades. This has happened to every sinner since the beginning of time. Hades is the realm of the dead to which sinners go when they die. No sinner will ever be released or escape from this place.

There is no other place that sinners go to when they die. Purgatory is a non-existent place. There is no scriptural basis for teaching that such a temporary place of suffering exists. Furthermore, people baptizing the living on behalf of the dead, in order to deliver them from a place of suffering, are deceived. It is also not true that the spirits of human beings can float around on the earth, as an ancestor. These are lies and deceptions of the devil himself. Those who die in their sins are immediately sucked down into Hades.

Job 12:14 ***If He imprisons a man, there can be no release.***

Hades is a place of no return but it is not the final destination of the sinner. It is merely *an awaiting trial jail* for all those who have died in sin. Hades is not Hell. Hell is the place that sinners are cast into after their judgment. This is the eternal prison and the final destination of sinners.

Everyone has the right to know about Hades and Hell. In this day and age it seems to be fashionable not to mention these places at all. There is no reason to hide this knowledge from anyone. Every preacher will give an account on whether they preached these truths or not.

The Lord Jesus Christ Himself saw it necessary, despite what modern preachers think, to set this extremely vivid picture of Hades before His hearers. The Holy Spirit captured it in the Word so that all generations could have this record. The entire portion of scripture is given below and must be read so that the reader can be fully informed.

> LUKE 16:19-31 ***There was a certain rich man who was clothed in purple and fine linen and fared sumptuously every day. But there was a certain beggar named Lazarus, full of sores, who was laid at his gate, desiring to be fed with the crumbs which fell from the rich man's table. Moreover, the dogs came and licked his sores. So it was that the beggar died, and was carried by the angels to Abraham's bosom. The rich man also died and was buried. And being in torments in Hades, he lifted up his eyes and saw Abraham afar off, and Lazarus in his bosom. Then he cried and said, 'Father Abraham, have mercy on me, and send Lazarus that he may dip the tip of his finger in water and cool my tongue; for I am tormented in this flame.' But Abraham said, 'Son, remember that in your lifetime you received your good things, and likewise Lazarus evil things; but now he is comforted and you are tormented. And besides all this, between us and you there is a great gulf fixed, so that those who want to pass from here to you cannot, nor can those from there pass to us.' Then he said, 'I beg you therefore, father, that you would send him to my father's house, for I have five brothers, that he may testify to them, lest they also come to this place of torment.' Abraham said to him, 'They have Moses and the prophets; let them hear them.' And he said, 'No, father Abraham; but if one goes to them from the dead, they will repent.' But he said to him, 'If they do not hear Moses and the prophets, neither will they be persuaded though one rise from the dead.'***

The above account is not some sort of fable or parable and must therefore be taken seriously. The rich man in the story above and, of course, the poor man, were definite people. This is proven to be so because the Lord said that, *"there was a certain rich man"* and not *"it was likened unto"* as He did when telling parables. These people had lived in or before the time of the Lord. The Lord must have seen the above in a vision and then related it to His hearers.

This account is about Hades, not Hell. Careful note must be taken of every detail. The rich man died but that was not the end of him. The beggar died but that was not the end of him either. The rich man, immediately after death, found himself in Hades. The poor man, whose name was Lazarus, floated down into a place, located directly across from Hades, but at somewhat of a distance to it, called Abraham's Bosom.

The rich man went to Hades not because he was rich and proud but because he died in his sins, and the poor man went to Abraham's Bosom not because he was poor and humble but because he believed in God.

The Lord continued with the account, and the horror that the rich man found himself in is very graphic. Immediately after death, the rich man found himself, "*in torments in Hades*". This means that he was in severe suffering, caused by the conditions that prevailed in this terrible place. Besides everything else that caused him to suffer, the torment of the perpetual flame that he was engulfed in caused unbearable anguish. Unlike the pleasant conditions that he had experienced on earth, where he could breathe easily, feel the cool morning breeze, be served delicious meals and reach out for a glass of cool water, here there was nothing but suffering. There were no streams, no afternoon refreshing showers of rain, no roses, no snow, no sea and no wells to draw water from. Here his tongue was forever parched by an unquenchable and increasing thirst.

The rich man was not alone in Hades. This was and still is the immediate but not final destination of all sinners. There were millions of others in this oppressive and unbearable place. They were all crying out for mercy and the rich man's torment was compounded by their never-ending, agonized screaming.

Directly across from where the rich man was confined was a place that the Lord Jesus called "Abraham's bosom". At some point in his suffering, the rich man lifted up his eyes and saw Abraham in the distance, together with all the righteous, including Lazarus, in this place of comfort and peace.

Suddenly, hope sprang up in his heart. Although, he knew that there was no escape from where he was, he still thought of the possibility of relief. This caused him to cry out to Abraham saying, *"Father Abraham, have mercy on me,"* and he begged him to send Lazarus to, "*dip the tip of his finger in water*" to cool his tongue because, he said, "*I am tormented in this flame*". Alas, his cry for mercy was too late. Mercy had been extended to him while he was alive. Abraham answered and said that that was impossible because there was *"a great gulf fixed, so that those who want to pass from here to you cannot, nor can those from there pass to us"*. There was an impassable divide between the righteous and the wicked dead, and the rich man's plea could not be granted.

The story continues and the rich man, in his suffering, began to wish his torment on none of his family. So he desperately cried out to Abraham to send somebody from the dead to warn his brothers and their families not to come to that place. Abraham's answer was direct. He said that no one would believe it, even if a person from the dead came to preach to them. Everyone had to listen to the Word of God. The rich man could only but turn away in despair and sink deeper into his torment. He is still there and so are millions of others.

Every sinner will remain in Hades until the last day. On that day, their bodies will be raised from the dead and will be united with their spirits that have been tormented in Hades all the time and they will be brought to their judgment.

JOHN 5:28-29 ***Do not marvel at this; for the hour is coming in which all who are in the graves will hear His voice and come forth – those who have***

done good, to the resurrection of life, and those who have done evil, to the resurrection of condemnation.

HEBREWS 9:27-28 ***And as it is appointed for men to die once, but after this the judgment, so Christ was offered once to bear the sins of many. To those who eagerly wait for Him He will appear a second time, apart from sin, for salvation.***

On that day, God will take His seat on what is described below as the *"Great White Throne"*. The glory of God will shine from the throne. Judgment day will have arrived. Awful terror will grip every sinner and they will at first flee in dread. This will be in vain because there will be no place to hide. John tried to describe the desperate and awful terror that will grip the universe but could only say that, *"heaven and earth fled away"*. Don't marvel at this either. It will happen because God said so.

The sinners will be rounded up and brought back to face their judgment. They will stand in the long line of the damned. Great and small will be there. Monarchs, nobles, prime ministers, presidents, geniuses, business moguls, authors and generals, as well as beggars, poor people, teachers, lawyers, doctors, sports people, priests and the like will be there. Every sinner who dies in their sins will be there.

God will open the books and will judge sinners out of there. The sins of sinners will roll up before their eyes and they will know that they are guilty. Their names will be sought in the Book of Life and will not be found. The reality of their final condemnation will hit them like a million bricks. This will be their final judgment. Read all about it in the Book of Revelations.

REVELATION 20:11-13 ***Then I saw a great white throne and Him who sat on it, from whose face the earth and the heaven fled away. And there was found no place for them. And I saw the dead, small and great, standing before God, and books were opened. And another book was opened, which***

is the Book of Life. And the dead were judged according to their works, by the things which were written in the books. The sea gave up the dead who were in it, and Death and Hades delivered up the dead who were in them. And they were judged, each one according to his works.

After they have been found guilty, they will bow their knees to the Lord Jesus Christ and confess Him as Lord.

PHILIPPIANS 2:10-11 ***... at the name of Jesus every knee should bow, of those in heaven, and of those on earth, and of those under the earth, and that every tongue should confess that Jesus Christ is Lord, to the glory of God the Father.***

The terror will not end there. Horror will engulf the condemned as they hear God commanding His angels to seize them, to bind their hands and their feet and to cast them into Hell.

MATTHEW 22:13 ***Bind him hand and foot, take him away, and cast him into outer darkness; there will be weeping and gnashing of teeth.***

Billions of the condemned will be cast down into the Lake of Fire that burns with fire and brimstone. An eternity of excruciating torment, accompanied with great weeping and continual grinding of teeth, will begin. The devil and all his demons will be there too, in torment. There will be no remission of sentence.

REVELATIONS 20:14-15 ***Then Death and Hades were cast into the lake of fire. This is the second death. And anyone not found written in the Book of Life was cast into the lake of fire.***

No sinner should allow himself to be deceived with persuasive words of man's wisdom. The wisdom of men is foolishness to God. Men profess themselves to be wise but in that they make themselves fools.

The truth is that, while modern men say that there is nothing to fear and others make a joke of it, sinners drop down into eternal damnation.

Hell is no joke. There is nothing funny about it. Nobody should laugh at foolish jokes about hell, made by careless sinners. One man said, "I will see what to do when I get there". By this he meant that he would argue his way out of his predicament when he came before God. This is a ridiculous statement. The truth is, heaven and earth will try to flee from the presence of God. Another said that, when he gets to the pearly gates of heaven, he will persuade Peter to let him in. That is only a joke. Nobody arrives at the gates of heaven seeking admittance. When sinners die, they get sucked down into Hades and stay there, in torment, until they are brought before the Great White Throne; after that they end up in Hell. This is no laughing matter at all.

Hades and Hell are real places. Many people in this day and age have been given visions of it. The Lord has taken them to the place and showed them the reality of it. These testimonies can be searched out on the Internet and books can be read about it. God brings the reality of it closer to home by giving people who live in these modern times experiences of Hades and Hell.

Finally, the above is not written to scare anybody, so that they can get saved. Fear will not get anybody into the Kingdom of God. However, the bad news must be presented before the good news can be received. The bad news is the devil and Hell and the good news is Jesus Christ and Heaven.

CHAPTER TWO

The Soul That Sins Shall Die

THE SOUL WHO SINS SHALL die. Almighty God said so Himself.

EZEKIEL 18:20 ***The soul who sins shall die.***

Now, what in the world could the above statement, *"The soul that sins shall die"*, mean? First, the word *"die"*, as used in the above scripture, could never simply mean the regular death that all people die when they reach the end of their lives. If this were the case then death would be a welcome relief for sinners. There would be absolutely nothing to fear. All people could sin at will throughout their lives and, when they die, all would be over.

1 CORINTHIANS 15:32 ***... If the dead do not rise, "Let us eat and drink, for tomorrow we die!"***

The emphatic way that God says this points to more than the natural death. He in fact refers to an eternal death. We now learn that this death is actually defined in the bible as the "second death".

REVELATION 20:14 ***Then Death and Hades were cast into the lake of fire. This is the second death.***

When God says, *"The soul who sins shall die,"* He in fact refers to this death. This is the death that the sinner will die. Dying a physical death only would merely amount to relief from this world's sufferings, but dying the second death would amount to an ultimate penalty. That is what it is: it is an ultimate penalty.

God declares several times in the Word of God that death is the ultimate penalty for sin. These scriptures must be read in the light of *"The soul who sins shall die"*.

First, God warned Adam that if he ever disobeyed Him and ate of the tree of the knowledge of good and evil, he would surely die. Adam did disobey God but he did not fall over and die. Was God wrong? The devil had said that they would not surely die if they disobeyed God. Was the devil right? Despite the devil's lie, this is what happened. After Adam sinned he did die, even if it happened thousands of years later. He died. He also died a spiritual death immediately, when his spirit was infused with the nature of sin. However, most importantly, he came under the condemnation of the second death, that he would die if he did not seek and receive the mercy of God. This is the ultimate penalty for sin.

> GENESIS 2:17 ***...but of the tree of the knowledge of good and evil you shall not eat, for in the day that you eat of it you shall surely die.***

Paul, who was well-schooled in the scriptures, set the ultimate penalty for sin in plain language. He said that the wages of sin is death. He could never have meant the natural death of the body because he was dealing with eternal realities. He later taught that the death that he was speaking about can be avoided if faith in Jesus Christ is exercised.

> ROMANS 6:23 ***For the wages of sin is death, but the gift of God is eternal life in Christ Jesus our Lord.***

James taught along the same lines. He spoke to people who already knew that everybody is subject to dying physically. The death that he was referring to is a death that is a result of practising sin.

James 1:14-15 ***But each one is tempted when he is drawn away by his own desires and enticed. Then, when desire has conceived, it gives birth to sin; and sin, when it is full-grown, brings forth death.***

The death referred to above is the ultimate penalty for sin. A divine penalty for sin can only mean that there is a divine government in place. This must be so because God rules the heavens and the earth. He has a divine government in place. Those who violate His righteous government will pay the ultimate penalty.

Ezekiel 18:20 ***The soul who sins shall die.***

Divine government is a reality and has a direct bearing on why people end up in Hell. It exists – and of that everyone can be absolutely sure. Everyone deep down inside knows that to be true and the scriptures testify to that very fact.

Isaiah 6:1 ***... I saw the Lord sitting on a throne, high and lifted up, and the train of His robe filled the temple.***

Revelation 4:3-5 ***... and He who sat there was like a jasper and a sardius stone in appearance; and there was a rainbow around the throne, in appearance like an emerald.... And from the throne proceeded lightnings, thunderings, and voices.***

God heads His government and He rules in almighty power. It is very clear to anyone who reads the scriptures above that, in any created world, God would be the ruler. God is the governor of heaven, earth and hell. How could it be otherwise?

To get a greater understanding of divine government, and why people are sent to Hell, one must realize that God is righteous. He is eternal and has many other attributes such as love, grace and mercy and all come to bear on His divine government but for now, only a focus on His righteousness is made.

> DANIEL 9:14 ***... for the Lord our God is righteous in all the works which He does,***

The law of God is based on His perfect righteousness. His righteousness is the rule of action by which we all must live. All the laws of God flow out of His eternal, righteous being. They have not been thought up by Him at some point in time, as some good idea. They are founded in His very being and cannot be changed. This is important for the sinner to grasp. God cannot change His righteous self for anyone. That is impossible.

For the benefit of human beings, God has spelled out His righteousness in laws such as, "thou shalt not murder", "thou shalt not steal", "thou shalt not covet" and a host of others throughout the bible. These laws are in place and really all point to the righteousness of God.

God has not only set His laws in place but has attached penalties for breaking the law. These must not be broken. If this is not true, then there would be no sense in having laws. Any violations of these laws are classified as crimes committed against God and His righteous government. It cannot be otherwise.

Sin and crime are synonymous terms. To commit a sin against God, is to commit a crime against God. God gives us this definition in the first letter of John.

> 1 JOHN 3:4 ***Whoever commits sin also commits lawlessness, and sin is lawlessness. (NKJV)***

The Old King James version of this scripture makes it even more clear. It defines sin as a transgression of the Law. To transgress a law is to violate that law and to violate a law is to commit a crime.

1 JOHN 3:4 ***Whosoever committeth sin transgresseth also the law: for sin is the transgression of the law. (KJV)***

The crux of the matter is this: whoever sins, violates the very righteousness of God. This is a crime against the divine government and the person who is guilty of this incurs the ultimate penalty, which is the second death.

CHAPTER THREE

The Soul That Sins Must Die

NOW COMES AN EVEN MORE serious matter. Every soul who sins must die. It must be so. If any person dies in his or her sins, God Himself *MUST* send that person to Hell. There are several reasons for this.

First, God's very own righteousness is at stake. If God allows sinners to get away with sin, then He will cease to be righteous and His kingdom will collapse. God cannot allow anyone to get away scot-free.

Second, God is God. He cannot allow some puny human being to sneeze at His existence. Humans are His creation and they must take Him into account. Rebellion against God cannot be tolerated. All rebels who refuse to repent must be rounded up and the sentence of death must be enforced. Rebels running around freely in the Kingdom of God? How can that be?

God's law is law. His law is not simply good advice or counsel for humans to live by. There are laws and there are penalties for breaking these laws. So, God must enforce them, if His government is to be taken seriously. There would be no sense in God having law, and penalties for breaking the law, yet not enforcing these. His government would then be treated as a toothless bulldog. Every sinner must know for certain that God will judge him or her after they die. God cannot allow anyone to sneer at His law.

The soul who sins must die because the eternal security of all the holy angels and the righteous is dependent on God enforcing His law. He is obligated to do so. All of heaven have their eyes on God and trust Him to act in line with His righteousness. He cannot allow His righteous government to collapse.

Sinners must be sent to a permanent place of confinement because their spirits have been defiled. Anyone who sins, persists and remains in sin until death, must be sent to a realm where all are of the same nature. The spirits of the defiled are treated like humans treat nuclear waste. They confine the waste to a particular protected area to prevent it from affecting its surroundings. Those who die with the nature of sin cannot be allowed to roam about the righteous kingdom of God.

EZEKIEL 18:20 ***The soul who sins shall die.***

Divine government is infinitely higher than any human government. No one who dies in their sins, can expect to escape the judgment of God. God's government is perfect. Every offender who ignores the grace of God and dies in his or her sins must be arrested, must be confined to Hades, must be brought before the Great White Throne, must be judged there, must be found guilty, must be bound hand and foot and must be cast into the Lake of Fire. It will not happen otherwise because God's *"legal system"* is tight.

REVELATION 20:14-15 ***Then Death and Hades were cast into the lake of fire. This is the second death. And anyone not found written in the Book of Life was cast into the lake of fire.***

Under human governments, those who commit crime may escape judgment and never end up in prison. We see this happen on a continual basis across the world. Some people who have committed crimes hide them and never end up in court. Others go to court but are never convicted because they have money and a sharp lawyer. Others get off with light, inappropriate sentences and are out among the community in a short space of time. This is why crime increases day by day.

This cannot happen under divine government. If God allows one offender to escape, then all can escape and crime will spread throughout His dominions. Chaos will be the result and the righteous government of God will collapse. God will cease to be God. Satan and sin will reign. So, it makes perfect sense that God cannot allow any angel or any man to go un-judged. *The soul that sins must die.*

The manner in which human governments work also proves why God must enforce His law. Every country has to have laws in place. This makes it possible for law and order to be enforced. This is an obvious truth. Then, of course, there must be penalties for breaking the law and there must be law enforcing agencies, if the government is to be taken seriously. If a law is broken, then the offender must be pursued, arrested and confined to a jail. The person must then be brought to trial. If the person is found guilty by a judge, an appropriate sentence must be passed. Prison authorities must then take the criminal into custody and imprison that person. These things must be so or there will be no government at all. A country that wishes to have peace within its borders must have a tight legal, justice and prison system in place. Justice must be seen to be carried out. If not, people will not take the government seriously. They will commit crimes with impunity and chaos and anarchy will reign.

Surely, the same must be allowed for divine government. A sinner who violates the righteousness of God must be arrested at death, must be confined to Hades, must be brought before the Great White Throne for judgement, must be sentenced and must then be confined to the eternal prison, Hell.

Sinners have committed crimes against the righteous government of God and they are therefore guilty. If they die in sin, they will still be guilty. Sinners cannot expect to die and be completely free from all judgement and retribution. No other understanding of the scriptures is possible.

CHAPTER FOUR

God Always Applies His Law

THE PENALTY FOR BREAKING THE law of God has always been applied: it is being applied right now and will always be applied. The examples below prove that this is true.

Take the issue of Lucifer first. When he and a certain group of angels rebelled against God, God enforced the law immediately. Their rebellion was a crime and this is what happened to them.

> LUKE 10:18 ***And He said to them, "I saw Satan fall like lightning from heaven".***

Lucifer and his fallen angels were in the very presence of the Holy Spirit when they chose to rebel. They were fully aware of the consequences, yet they chose the path of evil. There is no atonement for them and their ultimate destination will be the Lake of Fire, which is the second death.

> REVELATION 20:14 ***Then Death and Hades were cast into the lake of fire. This is the second death.***

> MATTHEW 25:41 ***... everlasting fire prepared for the devil and his angels.***

Likewise, when God placed Adam in the Garden of Eden, He warned him of the consequences of sin. He told him that if he sinned then, he would "*surely die*".

GENESIS 2:15-17 ***Then the Lord God took the man and put him in the garden of Eden to tend and keep it. And the Lord God commanded the man, saying, "Of every tree of the garden you may freely eat; but of the tree of the knowledge of good and evil you shall not eat, for in the day that you eat of it you shall surely die."***

When they unfortunately sinned, Adam and Eve did not fall over and die immediately. When they sinned they died an immediate spiritual death, came under the condemnation of the second death and eventually died physically. They would have to die the second death if they'd neglected the grace of God.

After Adam and Eve sinned, some people who were born thereafter looked to God for salvation and others rejected God. Those who rejected God have ended up in Hades (called Sheol in the Hebrew language). Their final destination is Hell. Those who died having faith in God have gone to the place of comfort directly across from Hades called Abraham's Bosom. Nobody has gone anywhere else. God has applied His law to everyone.

After the Lord Jesus Christ rose from the dead, God applied His law just as He has always done. Everyone who died in sin was sucked into Hades. They joined all those who had died in sin since the time of Adam and Eve. Those who died believing in Christ went to heaven. Nobody went anywhere else. God continues to apply His law until this very day.

The same will apply to everyone who dies in sin. God never and could never allow anyone to bypass His laws. If God did not allow Lucifer to escape His judgment and did not allow the angels that sinned to get away, why would God allow you, the reader, to escape His judgment?

God did not allow anyone to escape when He destroyed the wicked in the days of Noah and, when God destroyed Sodom and Gomorrah, He left an example for all to see what happens to the ungodly.

1 Peter 2:4-6 ***For if God did not spare the angels who sinned, but cast them down to hell and delivered them into chains of darkness, to be reserved for judgment; and did not spare the ancient world, but saved Noah, one of eight people, a preacher of righteousness, bringing in the flood on the world of the ungodly; and turning the cities of Sodom and Gomorrah into ashes, condemned them to destruction, making them an example to those who afterward would live ungodly;***

The sinner must not accept that all is well while yet in sin. God will apply His law and of that all can be sure.

CHAPTER FIVE

The Soul Who Sins Need Not Die

FORTUNATELY FOR US ALL, THERE is good news. Another aspect of God's government will immediately interest every sinner who wants to be saved. There is something called the *spirit of the law*. It is deeper and more powerful than the letter of the law.

2 CORINTHIANS 3:6 ***...who also made us sufficient as ministers of the new covenant, not of the letter but of the Spirit; for the letter kills, but the Spirit gives life***

The spirit of the law provides for atonement to be made for the sinner. If this is done, then God can safely extend mercy to the sinner without Himself being found guilty of breaking His own law. The letter of the law says that "*the soul who sins shall die*" but the spirit of the law says, "*because in His forbearance God had passed over the sins that were previously committed*". This means that the spirit of the law allows that, if atonement is made for the sinner, the soul who sins NEED NOT die.

God's law stands absolutely sure and unchangeable before every sinner. All humans have sinned and stand condemned before the eternal holy law of God.

ROMANS 3:23 ***...for all have sinned and fall short of the glory of God***

The letter of the law demands that *the soul who sins must die*. The law has no mercy: it condemns and demands justice. However, the spirit of the law makes a way where there seemed to be no way, and gives hope to the sinner. The spirit of the law triumphs over the letter of the law. *The soul who sins need not die*. Nobody needs to die the second death. Praise His holy name now and for evermore!

If atonement is the answer to the sinner's eternal woes, then all must, without delay, search out the meaning of it.

Atonement essentially means that someone qualified to do so can pay a price for sin and, if this is done, then God can release condemned sinners from judgment. This great truth is contained in the third chapter of Romans.

> ROMANS 3:25 ***...whom God set forth as a propitiation by His blood, through faith, to demonstrate His righteousness, because in His forbearance God had passed over the sins that were previously committed.***

This verse might be "complete Greek" to many, but a simple explanation makes it all clear. The scripture essentially means that the Lord Jesus Christ, through the shedding of His blood on the cross, removed the obstacle that prevented God the Father from overlooking the sins that sinners have committed. The shed blood of the Lamb of God allows God to remain righteous when He passes over the sins of those who put faith in His Son.

This is magnificent, wonderful, marvellous, splendid good news for the guilty sinner. This is huge, enormous, gargantuan, humungous good news for the condemned sinner. Wow! And why? Well, now all those who believe can escape the eternal damnation of the second death. Where there seemed to be no way, God has made a way.

My paraphrase of Romans 3:25 given above, lines up with the Amplified Version of the bible.

> ROMANS 3:25 ***Whom God put forward [before the eyes of all] as a mercy seat and propitiation by His blood [the cleansing and life-giving sacrifice of atonement and reconciliation, to be received] through faith. This was***

> ***to show God's righteousness, because in His divine forbearance He had passed over and ignored former sins without punishment. (Amplified)***

The last portion of the verse above says, *"He had passed over and ignored former sins without punishment"*. That must be clear to any reader who understands the English language. God has passed over sins without punishment! How did He do that and still remain righteous? He provided His Son as atonement. Glory be to God!

The Atonement

The meaning of atonement is set out below. In this we all rejoice. If sinners follow the directions given in this book, they will say the same thing that the psalmist said in the book of Psalms.

> PSALM 124:6-8 ***Blessed be the Lord, Who has not given us as prey to their teeth. Our soul has escaped as a bird from the snare of the fowlers; The snare is broken, and we have escaped. Our help is in the name of the Lord, Who made heaven and earth.***

Humankind had sinned and had come short of the glory of God. They could not do anything to save themselves. They were without hope and without God in a lost and dying world. They were like sheep without a shepherd wandering aimlessly on the hills. Hell was their eventual destination. There seemed to be no help.

> EPHESIANS 2:12 ***...that at that time you were without Christ, being aliens from the commonwealth of Israel and strangers from the covenants of promise, having no hope and without God in the world.***

However, God in His wonderful mercy, had a plan of salvation. A decision was taken to send His only begotten Son to the earth to save whoever would believe.

JOHN 3:16 ***For God so loved the world that He gave His only begotten Son, that whoever believes in Him should not perish but have everlasting life.***

The coming of the Son of God to this earth is a wonderful story. It is, in fact, the greatest story ever told. It needs an eternity to tell all its wonder. However, the story must of necessity be shortened.

A divine executive meeting was held in heaven to consider the sins of humankind. There the hopelessness of the world was considered. The second person of the Godhead, whom we know now as Jesus Christ said, "I will go!"

HEBREWS 10:5-7 ***Sacrifice and offering You did not desire, But a body You have prepared for Me. In burnt offerings and sacrifices for sin You had no pleasure. Then I said, "Behold, I have come—In the volume of the book it is written of Me—To do Your will, O God."***

Then, by a miracle, He was conceived in the womb of a virgin. There He took on flesh and blood and was born into this world.

JOHN 1:1,7 ***In the beginning was the Word, and the Word was with God, and the Word was God... And the Word became flesh and dwelt among us, and we beheld His glory, the glory as of the only begotten of the Father, full of grace and truth.***

He lived for about thirty-three and a half years on the earth and performed many miracles by the power of the Holy Spirit. He then turned His eyes from His earthly ministry and began to focus on His journey to the cross.

Motivated by jealousy, the religious establishment of the day had Him arrested and the Romans condemned Him to death. They beat Him up and whipped Him. After that, they took Him to a hill called Golgotha and there they crucified Him. He died and was buried in a tomb. However, on the third day, He was seen alive by many and then after forty days they saw Him ascend to heaven.

This is what the natural eye saw. However, after the Holy Spirit was sent from heaven, He revealed what really took place in the coming, crucifixion, death, burial, suffering, resurrection, ascension and exaltation of the Lord Jesus Christ.

The person Whom we know as the Lord Jesus Christ was none other then the second person of the eternal God, who took on flesh and blood. As a man, He was known as the Lamb of God. He walked on this earth for thirty-three and a half years and was tempted by the devil in all points, but never sinned. He was the perfect sacrifice because He was pure and holy.

> HEBREWS 4:15 ***For we do not have a High Priest who cannot sympathize with our weaknesses, but was in all points tempted as we are, yet without sin.***

The Lord allowed the wicked priests of Jerusalem to condemn Him to death, because He purposefully aimed to die the death of the cross. He knew that for this purpose He had come to the earth. When they crucified Him, unbeknown to His murderers, He was laying down His life for the world.

The above is what the natural eye could see. However, the scriptures go deeper and tell us what happened in the spiritual world. We start in Romans.

> ROMANS 5:25 ***...who was delivered up because of our offences, and was raised because of our justification***

This scripture explains it all. He *"was delivered up for our offences"*. Humans committed the offences against the righteous government of God and deserved to die the second death but He took their place and paid the price for their offences. The suffering of the righteous One in our place satisfied the righteous requirements of the Law. "*He was raised for our justification*", means that, in His resurrection, we could be set in right-standing with God. Hear what Isaiah says:

> ISAIAH 53:4-5 ***Surely He has borne our griefs and carried our sorrows; Yet we esteemed Him stricken, Smitten by God, and afflicted. But He was wounded for our transgressions, He was bruised for our iniquities; The chastisement for our peace was upon Him, And by His stripes we are healed.***

Anyone can see clearly how He took our place. *"He has borne our griefs and carried our sorrows"*. This is atonement. The righteous One bore the grief and sorrow of sin, which is the penalty for sin. He did this for us. We committed transgressions against the divine government and deserved the judgment of God but, *"He was wounded for our transgressions"*. This is atonement and, if understood, then the cross makes sense. He was wounded in order to shed His blood for us and that became a ransom price for our souls. *"He was bruised for our iniquities"* informs us that He took our place in the suffering of death so that we do not have to suffer for our sins. The same truth is revealed in the words, "*The chastisement for our peace was upon Him*".

There are other verses in this fifty-third chapter of Isaiah that make the fact of atonement clear to all.

> ISAIAH 53:6 ***And the Lord has laid on Him the iniquity of us all.***

> ISAIAH 53:8 ***For the transgressions of My people He was stricken.***

> ISAIAH 53:10 ***When You make His soul an offering for sin,***

> ISAIAH 53:11 ***My righteous Servant shall justify many, For He shall bear their iniquities.***

SAIAH 53:12 ***Because He poured out His soul unto death, And He was numbered with the transgressors, and He bore the sin of many, And made intercession for the transgressors.***

After the cross, and when the Spirit of God had come, He revealed to the apostles truths about the atonement that had been completed through the person and work of our Lord Jesus Christ. The letters to the church spell the atonement out clearly.

> 2 CORINTHIANS 5:21 ***For He made Him who knew no sin to be sin for us, that we might become the righteousness of God in Him***

It cannot be clearer. God provided atonement for us through the Lord Jesus Christ. God *"made Him who knew no sin to be sin for us"*. The righteous One who never committed sin, was made to be sin, *"for us"*. And God's intention was to make us the very *"righteousness of God"* Himself.

The same revelation is given to us through the apostle Peter.

> 1 PETER2:24 ***Who his own self bare our sins in his own body on the tree, that we, being dead to sins, should live unto righteousness: by whose stripes ye were healed.***

And also through John.

> 1 JOHN 2:2 ***And He Himself is the propitiation for our sins, and not for ours only but also for the whole world***

Here again it is: *"He...for our sins"*. God, through His Son and by the power of His Holy Spirit, has provided a full and complete atonement. The price for sin has been paid. Nobody needs to die the second death. If sinners follow what God tells them to do, He will waive the death penalty that hangs over their heads. The conditions are as clear as crystal in the scriptures. The soul that sins need not die.

CHAPTER SIX

Atonement

ATONEMENT MIGHT BE A DIFFICULT concept to understand for many but the short story given below might bring a better understanding of it.

John, a young man, was busy working on a farm when, in a moment of madness, he attacked the homestead of the owner of the farm. He burned down the farmer's house and his barns that were full of stored grain, killed his livestock and destroyed all his crops in the field. He then ran away.

The farmer was furious and was determined to have John arrested, and wanted him to receive a heavy sentence for his wicked deed. All the farmer's neighbours had their eyes set on the farmer. They knew that if the farmer did nothing about the wicked crime, then John would continue his deeds and others would follow suit. They felt that their entire peaceful and secure future depended on the farmer's actions.

When John's elder brother heard what his younger brother had done, he was moved with compassion for the farmer. However, he also loved his brother and knew that, even if he did fix up the farm, John would spend the rest of his life in prison because of the strict laws of that country. So he went to the farmer and offered to make amends. The farmer was still furious but afterwards relented.

The older brother then, at a complete cost to himself, rebuilt the farmer's house and all his barns. He built with great care and restored the buildings to an even greater glory than their former state. He then acquired livestock to replace what had been killed by John and restored them to the farm. He filled the barns with grain and ploughed the fields and sowed seed, so that fresh crops could grow. He repaired everything else that had been damaged by his younger brother. At the end of all his work, the farm was handed back to the farmer in pristine condition. The elder brother had spent every last cent he had to achieve this.

When the farmer saw what had been done, all anger subsided in him. The farmer said, "I am moved by all that you have done. You have perfectly satisfied the demands that I would have made on John. However, none of this could have been done by a neighbour and if they could, it would have counted for nothing. Only the reparation work of a brother would do. An elder brother has done it and has spent all that he had, so it counts for everything. You have made total reparation and I am now willing to and can forgive your brother. I want you to also know that all my neighbours wanted me to deal harshly with your brother, but now they are pleased that you have done this, allowing me to pass over his offence and to freely forgive him. Furthermore, I will ask the police to delay John's arrest, in the hope that he will come and ask me for forgiveness. As for you, who has done what no other man could do, I give you equal ownership of the farm, and I make you ruler over all my possessions and ask that you live here and be a son to me."

The elder brother then sent another brother, whom he had helped in the past, to go and tell John, who had committed such a horrible crime, that he, the elder brother, had done a complete work of reparation and that if he came and asked the farmer for forgiveness, he would be forgiven.

When the younger brother, who was completely destitute at that time and labouring under great guilt, heard what had been done, he amazingly would not return to ask for forgiveness. However, his brother did not take no for an answer, but brought him to the horizon of the farm, and showed him the perfect restoration work that his elder brother had done. He also showed him the smiling farmer seated on his huge chair on the porch of the house.

The wise brother even took his brother closer to hear a conversation between the elder brother and the farmer. He listened closely as he heard the farmer talk: "You have done a complete work of restoration. There is nothing that your brother still needs to do. All that he has to do is to turn away from his wicked ways, see and believe that you have done this wonderful work and say that you truly deserve to be the ruler of all and I will forgive him. I still love him and have always loved him. I long to have him back on the farm and wish he would come."

When the younger brother heard all this, he broke down and came out of the bushes, bowed his knee before his elder brother, who was now ruler of all, and sought forgiveness from the farmer. The farmer forgave John.

As it turned out, the farmer was, indeed, his very own father. The farmer invited John into the new house, bathed him, gave him perfumes, dressed him up in a Versace suit and threw a great big party for him.

CHAPTER SEVEN

The Sinner's Guilt

EVERY PERSON WHO IS ALIVE today, was born some time in this or in the last century or by some grace of great longevity, in the nineteenth century – and God have mercy on us all if someone who is still alive today was born in the eighteenth century. When they were born, their mothers held them in their arms and looked into their big innocent eyes.

Each person is born innocent. No one is born a guilty sinner. This is true because a first sin is always committed. Although the sin principle does lurk in the flesh, it is still the person who commits the first sin, and who is responsible for committing that sin. Sin is a person's choice and is a crime committed against God. A new-born babe cannot, therefore, be condemned at birth because it has not intentionally committed a sin. The bible teaches very clearly that every baby that is born into this world does not know the difference between good and evil.

DEUTERONOMY 1:39 ***Moreover your little ones and your children, who you say will be victims, who today have no knowledge of good and evil, they shall go in there; to them I will give it, and they shall possess it. But as for you, turn and take your journey into the wilderness by the Way of the Red Sea.***

ISAIAH 7:15-16 ***Curds and honey He shall eat, that He may know to refuse the evil and choose the good. For before the Child shall know to refuse the***

evil and choose the good, the land that you dread will be forsaken by both her kings.

After an innocent child is born into this world, it grows up rapidly and, in what usually seems to be a blink of an eye, there is one candle on the birthday cake. At that stage of the person's life, he or she is totally innocent. This means that if the baby should die, it would go straight to heaven. To continue, the little child has a second, a third and a fourth birthday party. The person continues to be innocent, even though he or she might do things that are apparently wrong. This is because the wrong doing still has no moral character. However, when the person reaches the age of accountability, which is somewhere between four and six years old, he or she sins intentionally. The sin could be the telling of a lie, stealing something, bursting out into selfish anger, acting spitefully, yielding to jealously or doing whatever is contrary to the Word of God. The innocent person is tempted, yields to the temptation and with purpose commits the foul deed.

JAMES 1:14-15 ***But each one is tempted when he is drawn away by his own desires and enticed. Then, when desire has conceived, it gives birth to sin; and sin, when it is full-grown, brings forth death.***

A person commits his or her first sin. The blame for this cannot be put on somebody else. The individual, and only the individual, is responsible and guilty for committing that sin.

Unfortunately, the foul deed of sin committed is not just an act that is morally wrong and that counts against the person's character; it is a crime committed against God. This is what the deed is. It cannot be viewed otherwise. The sin that is committed is a serious offence and a violation of the law of God.

1 JOHN 3:4 ***Whosoever committeth sin transgresseth also the law: for sin is the transgression of the law. (Old King James Version)***

Before continuing with the sad story, the horror of a sinful deed committed must be set forth, in clear terms. The true nature is amplified when one pauses for a moment to meditate on its horrible character. Sin is a violation of the law of God. Every sin is not necessarily one of the sins that follow here, however, it is *of the same nature* as the rape of an innocent woman, the forced entry into someone's home, the gunpoint robbery of an unsuspecting person or the cold-blooded murder of some person. It is a serious crime, committed in the very sight of the Judge, with a blatant disregard for any ramifications and consequences. The hideousness of sin is that every sin is a selfish and intentional act. A lie is committed to protect oneself at the expense of another. Theft is for personal gratification but injures another. Spitefulness inflicts harm on another person. Contemplating the horror of sin brings out its true character.

We must now return to the innocent person who committed his or her first sin. This person became guilty. It does not matter how small the sin may have appeared, the fact remains that the person was and still is guilty of committing a crime against God. This is if the person is still in sin.

> JAMES 2:10-11 ***For whoever shall keep the whole law, and yet stumble in one point, he is guilty of all. For He who said, "Do not commit adultery," also said, "Do not murder." Now if you do not commit adultery, but you do murder, you have become a transgressor of the law.***

> ROMANS 3:19 ***Now we know that whatever the law says, it says to those who are under the law, that every mouth may be stopped, and all the world may become guilty before God.***

Sad to say, the person did not stop there. Once the conscience was calmed, he or she ventured into another sin and then into another. As the person grew older, more sins were committed. The person might have ventured into pornography, fornication, homosexuality or even into adultery. He or she disregarded God and continued into pride, deception, vulgar language and maybe into violence and even into murder. The person did such things until his or her sins piled up, and became higher than the mountains.

This person is, as is everyone else, guilty and remains guilty while salvation is being neglected. Every person who dies in sin is guilty and will ever be so while being locked up in the *awaiting trial jail*, Hades.

CHAPTER EIGHT

False Hopes

MILLIONS UPON MILLIONS OF PEOPLE sense that something is wrong and they then try to get on the right side of God by getting themselves involved in some sort of religious activity. By this they hope to gain eternal life. However, after they die, they end up in Hell. Several of these false hopes are dealt with in this chapter.

Trying to keep the *law of Moses* gives people a false hope of salvation. Those who follow this system will never end up in heaven. The whole religious rigmarole is nothing but dead works, and is described as such in the bible.

> HEBREWS 6:1 ***...repentance from dead works***

Paul dealt with this extensively in his letters to the churches. He had deep compassion for the Jews at Rome. They had a zeal for God but were totally ignorant of the fact that only faith in Jesus Christ could bring righteousness.

> ROMANS 10:1-4 ***Brethren, my heart's desire and prayer to God for Israel is that they may be saved. For I bear them witness that they have a zeal for God, but not according to knowledge. For they being ignorant of God's righteousness, and seeking to establish their own righteousness, have not submitted to the righteousness of God. For Christ is the end of the law for righteousness to everyone who believes.***

The scripture in Philippians is direct.

PHILIPPIANS 3:3-9 ***For we are the circumcision, who worship God in the Spirit, rejoice in Christ Jesus, and have no confidence in the flesh, though I also might have confidence in the flesh. If anyone else thinks he may have confidence in the flesh, I more so: circumcised the eighth day, of the stock of Israel, of the tribe of Benjamin, a Hebrew of the Hebrews; concerning the law, a Pharisee; concerning zeal, persecuting the church; concerning the righteousness which is in the law, blameless. But what things were gain to me, these I have counted loss for Christ. Yet indeed I also count all things loss for the excellence of the knowledge of Christ Jesus my Lord, for whom I have suffered the loss of all things, and count them as rubbish, that I may gain Christ and be found in Him, not having my own righteousness, which is from the law, but that which is through faith in Christ, the righteousness which is from God by faith;***

Sadly, many who claim to be followers of this religion, also practise sins like adultery, abuse of alcohol, telling lies, stealing, curses and vulgar language, and so on. It is impossible, even if working for their own righteousness was right, for anyone to be in right-standing with God with such a life style.

People who claim to believe in Christ Jesus, and who are convinced that, in addition to following Christ, the keeping of the *Sabbath* is necessary to complete their righteousness, have a false hope of salvation. This is a futile exercise. The Sabbath was given only to the Jews and only until it was fulfilled by the Lord. In any case, nobody was and is able to keep it.

GALATIANS 2:21 ***"I do not set aside the grace of God; for if righteousness comes through the law, then Christ died in vain."***

COLOSSIANS 2:14-18 ***...having wiped out the handwriting of requirements that was against us, which was contrary to us... So let no one judge you in food or in drink, or regarding a festival or a new moon***

or sabbaths, which are a shadow of things to come, but the substance is of Christ. Let no one cheat you of your reward...

Trusting that *church membership* will get one into heaven is also a false hope of salvation. Someone may rightly say, "How on earth can one get to heaven just because of church membership?" Church membership cannot make one a Christian. Belonging to a church just because one's parents belonged to it does not get anyone in right-standing with God. This is common sense. Millions fill in forms that ask for their religious affiliation and declare that they are Christians, just because they grew up in a particular church. This a false hope of salvation.

I was a member of a church and considered myself a Christian, and so did most of the community in which I lived. However, most of the choir members of the church were very fond of their intoxicating drinks and indulged in these after Sunday morning church services. As a little boy, I would hear them use vulgar language and plan sinful romantic liaisons, and sometimes I would witness brutal brawls break out between these "Christians" and other members of the community. So much for their claim that they were Christians.

The only way to become a Christian is to repent, believe the gospel, confess Jesus Christ as Lord and to have corresponding faith actions.

JOHN 14:6 ***Jesus said to him, "I am the way, the truth, and the life. No one comes to the Father except through Me."***

It is a false hope of salvation to believe that one is in right-standing with God just because one was sprinkled as a baby, confirmed as a member of a church, confessed sins to a priest, was served what is called communion or gave reverence to high standing religious figures in the church. Reason must prevail. How could this wash away one's sins? Nothing can wash away our sins but the precious blood of Jesus Christ.

1 PETER 1:18-19 ***knowing that you were not redeemed with corruptible things, like silver or gold, from your aimless conduct received by tradition from your fathers, but with the precious blood of Christ, as of a lamb without blemish and without spot.***

All those who claim to be members of a church and still live a life of sin and are told that all is well, as long as they do not over do it, will perish in their sins.

2 TIMOTHY 2:19 ***Nevertheless the solid foundation of God stands, having this seal: "The Lord knows those who are His," and, "Let everyone who names the name of Christ depart from iniquity."***

Doing good works like feeding and clothing the poor, visiting the sick, helping the disadvantaged, building churches, hospitals or the like can never produce salvation. Those who set their hearts on such good works have a false hope of salvation. Salvation is a gift. There are no works that one can do that will result in a sinner earning salvation. If that were possible, there would have been no need for the cross.

EPHESIANS 2:8-9 ***For by grace you have been saved through faith, and that not of yourselves; it is the gift of God, not of works, lest anyone should boast.***

Many people diligently follow their religious convictions and hope to be included in the 144 000 people whom they believe will end up in heaven. Failing this, they hope that God will remember them and raise them from the dead. This is a false hope and they will perish in their sins. All believers have a promise to go to heaven when they die.

2 CORINTHIANS 5:8 ***We are confident, yes, well pleased rather to be absent from the body and to be present with the Lord.***

In some religious circles, leaders go to great lengths, baptizing people on behalf of those who have died. They believe that this ceremony will bring salvation to the dead. This is a false hope of salvation.

Those who put their trust in Mohammed, Confucius, Buddha, Krishna or any such leaders have a false hope of salvation.

> ACTS 4:12 ***Nor is there salvation in any other, for there is no other name under heaven given among men by which we must be saved."***

It is a false hope to believe that one can be saved through any traditional religion just because it has the word "Christian" added to its name. One cannot hope to be saved by trying to be a Christian and at the same time following witchcraft.

There are many different false hopes that people set their hearts on but they are too numerous to mention here.

The sinner must not allow himself or herself to be deceived. God is the one who in the end must be faced. Man's opinions must be rejected, abandoned, and the Word of God must be accepted. He is the One who said, *"The soul who sins shall die,"* and only His word will stand in the end.

CHAPTER NINE

Grace and Works

A GREAT MANY PEOPLE ARE caught up trying to earn salvation by doing good works. This is also a false hope of salvation that ties up many people in deception. It is dealt with in detail in this separate chapter.

We are all saved by grace. Nobody can be saved by doing good works. Paul makes that clear in his letter to the Ephesians and the scripture is self-explanatory.

> EPHESIANS 2:8 ***...by grace you have been saved through faith, and that not of yourselves; it is the gift of God, not of works, lest anyone should boast.***

Salvation is a gift of God. It is by grace and is appropriated by faith. It is as simple as that. One just reaches out by faith and takes it, as one would receive any other gift. For example, if a person is handed a watch as a gift, no effort to earn it is required by the recipient. All that the person has to do is to reach out and receive the gift.

If anyone could be saved by doing good works, then there would be no need for Christ Jesus and for His work of atonement. In the light of the fact of the atonement, salvation can only be by grace. Salvation can only be a gift because it is the Lord Jesus Christ who paid the price for sin and it is therefore God's prerogative to give the gift to whomever He decides to give it to.

Paul says that it is, *"not of yourselves"*. This is true because it cannot be by works because then people would boast. Humans would claim the glory and the substitutionary sacrifice of the life of the Lord Jesus Christ would have been unnecessary. How could this ever be?

If salvation could be achieved by doing good works and if this was required of the sinner, the question has to be asked: how much good work would be necessary? Nobody can answer that question in a satisfactory manner. The tormenting question will always persist – "Did I do enough?" – and the Word of God will ever answer, "Nobody could ever do enough, even if they tried".

> ISAIAH 64:5 ***But we are all like an unclean thing, And all our righteousnesses are like filthy rags; We all fade as a leaf, And our iniquities, like the wind, Have taken us away.***

Trying to attain salvation by works is like someone attempting to jump from a dock in Cape Town and wanting to land on Australian soil. The biggest jump will only result in the person ending up in the water directly below them. We all fall far short of what is required of us.

> ROMANS 3:23 ***...for all have sinned and fall short of the glory of God,***

It is an absolute impossibility to be saved by doing the good works required by the Law of Moses, therefore Christ came to die for us all.

> GALATIANS 2:21 ***I do not set aside the grace of God; for if righteousness comes through the law, then Christ died in vain.***

To try to earn salvation through works is to set aside God's grace that has already been given. The person who does this acts towards the grace of God as though it has been abolished and thwarts the efficacy of His grace.

Many people preach that Christ died for their sins but then try to add works as a religious activity that is supposed to be a necessity for salvation. How this can add to the perfect salvation that Christ has already provided remains a mystery. The fundamental meaning of grace is that salvation is given free, without money and without price.

> GALATIANS 2:16 ***...knowing that a man is not justified by the works of the law but by faith in Jesus Christ, even we have believed in Christ Jesus, that we might be justified by faith in Christ and not by the works of the law; for by the works of the law no flesh shall be justified.***

It is very easy to get saved. God makes it easy but humans are the ones who complicate it. Salvation is a gift and is simply received by faith. There is no need for a long works programme that might lead to salvation. The Word of God puts it on a gift basis. There are many scriptures that are in the bible that prove that one is saved by grace. One cannot expound on each but they are listed below and the reader can read each one.

> ROMANS 5:6-8 ***For when we were still without strength, in due time Christ died for the ungodly. For scarcely for a righteous man will one die; yet perhaps for a good man someone would even dare to die. But God demonstrates His own love toward us, in that while we were still sinners, Christ died for us.***

> TITUS 3:5-7 ***...not by works of righteousness which we have done, but according to His mercy He saved us, through the washing of regeneration and renewing of the Holy Spirit, whom He poured out on us abundantly through Jesus Christ our Saviour, that having been justified by His grace we should become heirs according to the hope of eternal life.***

> JOHN 6:28-29 ***Then they said to Him, "What shall we do, that we may work the works of God?" Jesus answered and said to them, "This is the work of God, that you believe in Him whom He sent."***

2 CORINTHIANS 5:21 ***For He made Him who knew no sin to be sin for us, that we might become the righteousness of God in Him.***

EPHESIANS 1:7 ***In Him we have redemption through His blood, the forgiveness of sins, according to the riches of His grace***

1 TIMOTHY 1:15-16 ***This is a faithful saying and worthy of all acceptance, that Christ Jesus came into the world to save sinners, of whom I am chief. However, for this reason I obtained mercy, that in me first Jesus Christ might show all long-suffering, as a pattern to those who are going to believe on Him for everlasting life.***

ACTS 4:12 ***Nor is there salvation in any other, for there is no other name under heaven given among men by which we must be saved.***

ROMANS 5:15-17 ***But the free gift is not like the offence. For if by the one man's offence many died, much more the grace of God and the gift by the grace of the one Man, Jesus Christ, abounded to many. And the gift is not like that which came through the one who sinned. For the judgment which came from one offence resulted in condemnation, but the free gift which came from many offences resulted in justification. For if by the one man's offence death reigned through the one, much more those who receive abundance of grace and of the gift of righteousness will reign in life through the One, Jesus Christ.***

This should settle the matter for any honest seeker of truth.

James 2:14-26

There is a scripture in the book of James that must be studied when teaching that we are saved by grace and grace alone. The passage is found in the second chapter of the Book of James. The entire scripture is given below for careful study.

James 2:14–26 ***What does it profit, my brethren, if someone says he has faith but does not have works? Can faith save him? If a brother or sister is naked and destitute of daily food, and one of you says to them, "Depart in peace, be warmed and filled," but you do not give them the things which are needed for the body, what does it profit? Thus also faith by itself, if it does not have works, is dead. But someone will say, "You have faith, and I have works." Show me your faith without your works, and I will show you my faith by my works. You believe that there is one God. You do well. Even the demons believe—and tremble! But do you want to know, O foolish man, that faith without works is dead? Was not Abraham our father justified by works when he offered Isaac his son on the altar? Do you see that faith was working together with his works, and by works faith was made perfect? And the Scripture was fulfilled which says, "Abraham believed God, and it was accounted to him for righteousness." And he was called the friend of God. You see then that a man is justified by works, and not by faith only. Likewise, was not Rahab the harlot also justified by works when she received the messengers and sent them out another way? For as the body without the spirit is dead, so faith without works is dead also.***

This passage of scripture is a problem to many readers. They think wrongly and believe wrongly, and this they do to the eternal damnation of their souls.

James is inspired by the Holy Spirit and must be right. The problem is finding the correct interpretation of this passage. This is done and made easy when it is interpreted in the light of other scripture.

The truth that we are saved by grace cannot be set aside. Salvation is a gift and the whole message of the New Testament is that Christ died a vicarious death for us all. James may not, cannot and does not teach that *good works* are necessary to achieve salvation. He does, however, teach that *faith works* are indispensable to salvation.

James teaches *faith works,* or we may say *works of faith.* Take for example the accompanying works that perfected Abraham's faith. These were not good works. These were faith works. Abraham went to the mountain to sacrifice his son. His claim to faith would mean nothing without these corresponding actions. His faith works completed the faith that was in his heart.

> JAMES 2:21-24 ***Was not Abraham our father justified by works when he offered Isaac his son on the altar? Do you see that faith was working together with his works, and by works faith was made perfect? And the Scripture was fulfilled which says, "Abraham believed God, and it was accounted to him for righteousness." And he was called the friend of God. You see then that a man is justified by works, and not by faith only.***

What appears to be a difficult passage above, turns out not to be really so. A closer study of the word *justified* clears up further wrong thinking. James could not have been speaking about New Testament salvation justification here, because he knew that a sinner could only be justified by the precious blood of the Lord Jesus Christ. The word *justified,* as used here, can only mean that Abraham was proven to have a living faith by his actions.

Furthermore, the works spoken of by James are not good works that humans try to do in order to get saved. If the impossible goal of pursuing salvation by good works is embarked upon by a sinner, then the motive might be to skip the repenting, believing, confession and continuing parts of salvation. Feeding and clothing the poor comes *after* salvation and not *for* salvation.

> JAMES 2:15-17 ***If a brother or sister is naked and destitute of daily food, and one of you says to them, "Depart in peace, be warmed and filled," but you do not give them the things which are needed for the body, what does it profit? Thus also faith by itself, if it does not have works, is dead.***

In the portion of scripture above, James is simply saying that, just as it makes no sense to say to a needy person to go in the peace of God and not give them what they need, when it is within one's ability to do so, faith with no corresponding actions is dead. He is not trying to prove that feeding and clothing the poor is necessary for salvation.

In the scripture below, the problem of salvations by works is also cleared up, if a focus is put on the words "*thus also*". James is merely comparing the deadness of the person's compassion without works, to the deadness of faith without the corresponding actions. He says that faith is good but needs corresponding faith actions to give it life.

> JAMES 2:14,17 ***What does it profit, my brethren, if someone says he has faith but does not have works? Can faith save him?... Thus also faith by itself, if it does not have works, is dead.***

> JAMES 2: ***For as the body without the spirit is dead, so faith without works is dead also.***

James was aware of the fact that one is saved by grace because that is how he got saved. Here he was dealing with those who confess that Jesus Christ is Lord but have no lifestyle to prove it. James is correct because, if one is saved, then there will be corresponding actions that go with being born again. Nobody could be saved if they lived a habitual lifestyle of sin and were never convicted.

He was saying that it would be perfectly natural for the person who is saved to have evidence of salvation. Those who get saved, start going to church, they begin to pray, they praise God, they give, they live a holy life, they have compassion for the poor and do many such kinds of things. Thus James was teaching that, when there is genuine faith, the aforementioned *faith works* will be present.

> JAMES 2:17 ***Thus also faith by itself, if it does not have works, is dead.***

Faith actions give spirit and life to the faith. They drive faith and keep it alive. Corresponding faith works bring the salvation of the sinner to completion and to a well-rounded whole.

CHAPTER TEN

Disbelief in and Disregard for God

MANY PEOPLE DON'T BELIEVE THAT God exists and some wonder if He does. Then there are those who live very respectable lives, say that they believe that He exists, yet have nothing to do with Him at all. Many are just wild sinners who commit sin with brazenness but never outright deny the existence of God. However, in the final analysis, all of these, in word and deed, despise the Almighty.

An atheist denies the existence of God. Atheists cannot be saved while they persist in their position. God provides salvation and cannot give it to somebody who doesn't even believe that He exists. People who die as atheists end up in Hell.

PSALMS 14:1 ***The fool has said in his heart, "There is no God".***

An agnostic is unsure whether God exists or not. Agnostics cannot receive salvation because they doubt the existence of God. Agnostics who persist to the end in their folly will lose their precious souls.

HEBREWS 11:6 ***But without faith it is impossible to please Him, for he who comes to God must believe that He is, and that He is a rewarder of those who diligently seek Him.***

Some people live very respectable lives and have some acknowledgment of the existence of God. These people sometimes attend church gatherings and sit through some kind of church service, to salve their conscience, but in reality they do not believe in God at all. These kinds of people usually drink alcohol, use vulgar language when it suits them, they lie whenever they want to, hate people as they desire and generally live ungodly lives. In word and deed, they prove that they disregard God. All those who live such lives will perish in their sins.

Then there are sinners who don't care about God at all. They are wild sinners who commit sin at will. They might on rare occasions acknowledge that God exists but, at the first opportunity, plunge into sin again. Such kinds of people will also end up in Hell.

Nevertheless, none of these people will perish without a witness from God. The wonderful God Who freely provides salvation does not leave sinners to themselves. He is always busy proving His existence, so that people can reach out to Him.

God's first witness is found in His creation. It is a message to every person who lived, lives or will ever live. The wonder of it causes the observer to acknowledge that a divine hand was at work in the creation of all things. The vastness and glory of the universe proves that there is a God, and that He is almighty. There is nowhere in the world where His message is not understood.

> PSALM 19:1-4 ***The heavens declare the glory of God; And the firmament shows His handiwork. Day unto day utters speech, and night unto night reveals knowledge. There is no speech nor language where their voice is not heard. Their line has gone out through all the earth, and their words to the end of the world.***

God's very attributes can be seen by those who merely look at nature. The fact that He is eternal can be seen in everything that He made. The apple tree comes out the same every year and so does the lion at birth. Only an Almighty God could have created such a vast universe and be able to sustain it. A created universe with no omnipresent being cannot be. The hand of an omniscient God can be seen in the wonderful body and mind of man. From the intricate heart or the engineering miracle of the knee, the wisdom of God is clearly seen. His love, goodness, kindness, mercy and all His natural attributes are seen in nature. The proof is there every day and there is no excuse not to notice this.

> ROMANS 1:18-20 ***... what may be known of God is manifest in them, for God has shown it to them. For since the creation of the world His invisible attributes are clearly seen, being understood by the things that are made, even His eternal power and Godhead, so that they are without excuse***

At first, unbelieving scientists thought that creationists were just ignorant. However, now there are more and more creationist scientists who prove the existence of God. Unbelieving scientists stand mute when challenged with the law of angular motion. They have no answer to the fact that diamonds come from the centre of the earth and yet have carbon in them. They have no answer to drawings on cave walls of humans standing next to dinosaurs, who are supposed to have been extinct for millions of years. The list goes on and on.

God's demonstration of the supernatural is another way that He proves His existence. There are testimonies of healing and comings of people back to life who have died, that astound doctors. The casting out of demons proves that there is a spiritual world and that the name of Jesus prevails there. Countless visions of God have been granted to people of Heaven, of Hell and of the Lord Jesus Christ Himself. Providences in peoples lives cannot be explained away.

Unbelievers who think that they have time can work through the witness that God gives them. However, those who are eager to be saved, can dive right into faith.

CHAPTER ELEVEN

Salvation Received in an Instant

A SINNER GETS SAVED IN an instant. There is no long process of repentance, believing, confession or some sort of works programme. Every account of people getting saved that is recorded in the Book of Acts, proves that people got saved in an instant.

The first account that is looked at closely is the one that happened on the Day of Pentecost. As Peter preached, the people *"were cut to the heart"*. In their conviction they enquired of Peter and the rest of the apostles what they should do in order to be saved. Peter told them what to do and the people did what he said. They turned away from Judaism, believed and confessed Christ Jesus as Lord. So they got saved at that very moment. Their repentance, believing that atonement was provided for them through the finished work of Christ, their confession that He is Lord and the corresponding faith action of bowing the knee, all happened in an instant. Salvation was received as a gift, and had to be in a moment. The scripture makes it clear and informs us that it all happened on *"that day"*.

> ACTS 40:41 ***Then those who gladly received his word were baptized; and THAT DAY about three thousand souls were added to them.***

Philip's preaching at Samaria also resulted in instant salvations. The people immediately turned to the Lord when they believed. This is how it worked then and this is how it works now.

Acts 8:5,8,14 ***Then Philip went down to the city of Samaria and preached Christ to them. And the multitudes with one accord heeded the things spoken by Philip... And there was great joy in that city... Now when the apostles who were at Jerusalem heard that Samaria had received the word of God...***

Philip then went on, found an Ethiopian and preached the gospel to him. This man accepted Christ right there and then and was immediately baptized. The scripture makes it crystal clear that the Ethiopian's repentance, believing, confession and corresponding faith actions happened in a moment.

Acts 8:35,38,39 ***Then Philip opened his mouth, and beginning at this Scripture, preached Jesus to him.... And he answered and said, "I believe that Jesus Christ is the Son of God."... he baptized him. and he went on his way rejoicing.***

Paul, the apostle, received his salvation in the same way. When the Lord appeared to him on the way to Damascus, he believed immediately and in that moment confessed Christ as Lord. This means that he turned away from Judaism there and then and acted in faith. Salvation is a gift that is received in an instant.

Acts 9:3-6 ***As he journeyed he came near Damascus, and suddenly a light shone around him from heaven. Then he fell to the ground, and heard a voice saying to him, "Saul, Saul, why are you persecuting Me?" And he said, "Who are You, Lord?" Then the Lord said, "I am Jesus, whom you are persecuting. It is hard for you to kick against the goads." So he, trembling and astonished, said, "Lord, what do You want me to do?"***

Cornelius and his household also received salvation and the baptism in the Holy Spirit all in a moment. There is no argument against what

Peter said after members of Cornelius' household were filled with the Holy Spirit.

> ACTS 10:44-48 ***While Peter was still speaking these words, the Holy Spirit fell upon all those who heard the word. And those of the circumcision who believed were astonished, as many as came with Peter, because the gift of the Holy Spirit had been poured out on the Gentiles also. For they heard them speak with tongues and magnify God. Then Peter answered, "Can anyone forbid water, that these should not be baptized who have received the Holy Spirit just as we have?" And he commanded them to be baptized in the name of the Lord. Then they asked him to stay a few days.***

Lydia received her salvation in a moment, just as the others did.

> ACTS 16:15 ***Now a certain woman named Lydia heard us. She was a seller of purple from the city of Thyatira, who worshipped God. The Lord opened her heart to heed the things spoken by Paul. And when she and her household were baptized, she begged us, saying, "If you have judged me to be faithful to the Lord, come to my house and stay." So she persuaded us.***

Under Paul's ministry, the jailer and his family were also saved during the very night that he asked, *"Sirs, what must I do to be saved?"*

> ACTS 16:31-34 ***So they said, "Believe on the Lord Jesus Christ, and you will be saved, you and your household." Then they spoke the word of the Lord to him and to all who were in his house. And he took them the same hour of the night and washed their stripes. And immediately he and all his family were baptized. Now when he had brought them into his house, he set food before them; and he rejoiced, having believed in God with all his household.***

It is important to understand this concept if the teachings that lie ahead are to be understood. Many people think that when one speaks of repentance, it is meant that a lengthy process must be followed until a reasonable or perfect degree of holiness is affected in a person. After that, they think a person must spend time studying the word of God in order to believe. After this, they think that they must enter into some sort of ceremonial confession that is followed by doing good works. This, they think, will bring them into right-standing with God. This is not the case at all. Repentance, believing, confessing and a faith action all happen in an instant and result in salvation at that moment. In this book, repentance, believing, confession, corresponding faith actions are only separated for study purposes.

If a works programme that is a false hope is followed then, of course, the person who seeks to be saved will labour at it for the rest of his or her life. However, if salvation is received through grace then it will be received in an instant, because it is a gift.

CHAPTER TWELVE

The Sinner's Salvation

In various places in the bible sinners are told to repent, other places to believe, to confess Christ as Lord and in other places to have actions that correspond to faith. In order to explain this to both the sinner and the believer the concept of a *continuum* must be clearly set forth. This is because salvation is really a continuum. It consists of repentance, believing, confessing and corresponding faith actions. This is the best way to describe how salvation is received.

First, the concept of a continuum is not so difficult to understand. A little focusing of the mind and the definition that follows will make it clear.

A continuum is a continuous sequence, with adjacent elements that are not perceptibly different from each other, but each is nonetheless quite distinct, although one element cannot exist without the other and all make up a well rounded whole.

Repentance, believing, confession and corresponding faith actions make up the salvation continuum. They are very closely related and all happen together. To believe and to embrace the atonement is directly accompanied by a turning away from a false hope of salvation or disbelief in God. A confession that Christ is Lord is just the obverse side of the same coin. Corresponding faith actions mean that one has repented, believed and is confessing that Christ Jesus is Lord.

Receiving salvation happens like this many times. A person sits in a crowd while the gospel is being preached and believes. An altar call is made and the person gets up and goes to the front. When the person follows the preacher in prayer they are, in fact, turning away from false hopes of salvation or a disbelief in God. At that very moment they also believe and embrace the finished work of atonement made by the Lord Jesus Christ and make a confession that Christ Jesus is Lord. Their prayer, lifting up their hands in gratefulness and uttering their first hallelujah, are all corresponding faith actions that happen at that instant. It is as simple as that.

CHAPTER THIRTEEN

Repent

The first element of salvation is repentance. If anyone wants to get saved they must start here. Nobody can get into believing and confession without repentance. The order is clear in the bible. Repentance comes before faith.

> HEBREWS 6:1 ***... the foundation of repentance from dead works and of faith toward God...***

Everybody who ever got saved had to first repent. It cannot be otherwise. For the sinner's own good, God commands him or her to repent.

> ACTS 17:30 ***Truly, these times of ignorance God overlooked, but now commands all men everywhere to repent***

Repentance clears the way for believing the gospel. The sinner cannot hold the devil's tail with one hand, and the bible in the other, at the same time. A person who comes to church, praises God, and then goes down to a Hindu temple and engages in all the rituals there, cannot exercise true faith in Jesus Christ. Someone who is really impressed with the miracles of Christ and spends time with believers in church, yet goes down to the mosque on a Friday afternoon and bows down to worship Allah, cannot believe in and confess Christ Jesus as Lord at the same time. One cannot drink alcohol until one is drunk, swear, curse, lie and hate and then come to church every Sunday and claim to have true faith in Christ. No one can move in two opposite directions at the same time. The sinner must first repent and then exercise faith in God. To believe what Christ Jesus has done in His work of atonement, to confess Him as Lord and to have corresponding faith actions, is only possible if one genuinely repents.

God then demands a complete change of mind of the sinner's religious convictions or the lack of it. It is impossible for Him to grant remission of sins to anyone if the person is still serving a false god, pursuing a false religious system, living an habitual life of sin or if the person does not even believe that He exists. So, of necessity, the sinner must first make a 180 degree turn from his or her present spiritual position and then move on in faith. Examples of repentance in the book of Acts illustrate the kind of repentance that sinners made when they got saved.

The first instance is found in the second chapter of the Book of Acts. On the day of Pentecost, Peter preached to those standing before him. The crowd was made up of many religious Jews who were *"devout men, from every nation under heaven"*. Peter preached Christ to them. He did not demand that they turn from adultery, lies, stealing and the like. This would happen after they got saved, but the first issue that had to be dealt with was Jesus Christ. The choice that was set before these Jews was that they could either believe that Christ died a vicarious death for them and was then raised from the dead by God or continue in their bankrupt Judaism.

ACTS 2:38 ***Then Peter said to them, "Repent...***

More than three thousand decided to turn away from all that Judaism offered. This was their repentance. They had been trusting in the Law of Moses and all their religious duties as a means of getting into right standing with God but, when they realized that Jesus Christ was the saviour, they rejected the false hope that Judaism offered them. Their new life in Christ, described below, shows that a 180 degree turn away from Judaism was made. They were going one way but, in their repentance, they turned and went directly in the opposite direction.

> ACTS 2:41-47 ***Then those who gladly received his word were baptized; and that day about three thousand souls were added to them. And they continued steadfastly in the apostles' doctrine and fellowship, in the breaking of bread, and in prayers. Then fear came upon every soul, and many wonders and signs were done through the apostles. Now all who believed were together, and had all things in common, and sold their possessions and goods, and divided them among all, as anyone had need. So continuing daily with one accord in the temple, and breaking bread from house to house, they ate their food with gladness and simplicity of heart, praising God and having favour with all the people. And the Lord added to the church daily those who were being saved.***

This is the kind of repentance required from the sinner. One must turn away from every false hope of salvation, disbelief or disregard for God and turn to the Lord Jesus Christ.

Two examples are set forth in the ministry of Philip, the evangelist. First, Philip preached to the Samaritans. These were sinners who were taken in with the witchcraft of a certain Simon. If they were yielding to witchcraft, one can reasonably assume that other sins like lying, stealing, adultery and fornication, would be common among them. Philip did not demand a turning away from these types of sin but rather preached Christ to them.

> ACTS 8:4-6 ***Therefore those who were scattered went everywhere preaching the word. Then Philip went down to the city of Samaria and preached Christ to them. And the multitudes with one accord heeded the things spoken by Philip, hearing and seeing the miracles which he did.***

The repentance of these Samaritans is clear. They abandoned their old beliefs and they turned to Christ.

Second, Philip, after preaching at Samaria, went on further and met a certain Ethiopian on his way to Gaza. This is a very interesting account that is recorded in the eighth chapter of the book of Acts. A focus on the thirty-fifth verse must be made. Philip never required that the Ethiopian first turn away from all the sins he'd committed up to then, as a prerequisite for faith in Christ. He preached Christ to Him. This meant that if the Ethiopian believed in Christ, he would of necessity have to turn away from Judaism. He did and this was his repentance.

> ACTS 8:35 ***Then Philip opened his mouth, and beginning at this Scripture, preached Jesus to him.***

In the case of Paul, the apostle, we have the same introduction into the eternal life. Paul, who was called Saul at that time, heard the gospel from different quarters but the preaching of Stephen convinced him. Stephen preached Jesus Christ. Shortly after hearing the gospel of Jesus Christ, the Lord Himself appeared to Paul. This is what got Paul saved. He chose between Judaism and Jesus Christ. Paul decided to turn away from the false hope of salvation that the Jewish religion offered.

> ACTS 9:3-6 ***As he journeyed he came near Damascus, and suddenly a light shone around him from heaven. Then he fell to the ground, and heard a voice saying to him, "Saul, Saul, why are you persecuting Me?" And he said, "Who are You, Lord?" Then the Lord said, "I am Jesus, whom you are persecuting. It is hard for you to kick against the goads." So he, trembling and astonished, said, "Lord, what do You want me to do?"***

Paul also directed the jailer in Philippi to turn away from his old life and to turn to Christ. The jailer believed and was saved and baptized in water.

> ACTS 16:31 ***So they said, "Believe on the Lord Jesus Christ, and you will be saved, you and your household."***

One just has to look at what Paul preached to see that he preached Christ to the lost and expect his hearers to turn away from what they believed and to accept Jesus Christ as the saviour.

> ROMANS 1:16-17 ***For I am not ashamed of the gospel of Christ, for it is the power of God to salvation for everyone who believes, for the Jew first and also for the Greek. For in it the righteousness of God is revealed from faith to faith; as it is written, "The just shall live by faith."***

> 1 CORINTHIANS 1:18 ***For the message of the cross is foolishness to those who are perishing, but to us who are being saved it is the power of God.***

> 1 CORINTHIANS 2:2 ***For I determined not to know anything among you except Jesus Christ and Him crucified.***

In the final analysis, it is clear that repentance is a turning away from a false hope of salvation, a disregard and disbelief in God.

Well meaning people demand that the sinner turn away from sins like adultery, fornication, hatred, violence, addiction to alcohol, stealing, lying and the like in order to get saved. This cannot be what is required in repentance because if sinners only did that, they would end up being nothing more than reformed sinners and will, unfortunately, still end up in Hell. This kind of repentance can never get anybody saved because it lacks the elements of repentance from dead works. Believing in the finished work of Christ has no confession that Jesus Christ is Lord and has no corresponding faith works.

However, it is true that at the moment after salvation the new believer must immediately begin to turn away from everything that is contrary to the will of God. The above is proven in the experience of all those who are engaged in soul winning. When people are found or known to be living together in fornication or abusing drugs or living a wild life of sin, they are not directed to first set their lives *"right with God"* and then to accept Christ. They are led to Christ and encouraged to come to church. After that they are discipled.

Telling sinners to list the sins that they have committed in the past and to repent of them, one by one, in order to get saved is misdirected. This can never get anybody saved. The person who wants to get saved will never be able to remember all their sins. This is an obvious impossibility. The sinner who wants to be saved must turn away from all false hopes of salvation or disbelief in God, must believe that Christ made full atonement for them, must confess that Christ is Lord and they will be saved. A corresponding faith action, like lifting up holy hands and thanking God for their salvation, brings their faith to life.

The scripture that follows was written to Christians and not to sinners. Preachers have no business preaching this to the lost and misdirecting them as above.

> 1 JOHN 1:9 ***If we confess our sins, He is faithful and just to forgive us our sins and to cleanse us from all unrighteousness.***

The sinner's repentance is not the same as the born-again Christian's repentance. People who are saved have their whole body of sin washed away when they receive salvation. Sadly, after they get saved, they still commit sin, but then they need ask God forgiveness for those sins. This is not the case with the sinner.

Penance is a false doctrine that requires certain acts of self-discipline to prepare a sinner for salvation. No one needs to devote time to prayer, reading the bible, fasting or any other harder acts of self-discipline to prepare themselves for forgiveness. Nobody did that in the Book of Acts.

Nobody will ever get saved by confessing their sins to any human being. This is a futile exercise. The unsaved have no business confessing their sins to priests.

CHAPTER FOURTEEN

Believe

THE SECOND ELEMENT OF SALVATION is to believe. Although all the elements of salvation – namely repentance, believing, confession and a corresponding faith action – happen in an instant, believing is separated here, for easy study. At repentance the sinner enters into believing. The two scriptures below set out the elements of believing and confession. However, in this chapter, only the believing part is emphasized.

> ROMANS 10:9-10 ***...that if you confess with your mouth the Lord Jesus and believe in your heart that God has raised Him from the dead, you will be saved. For with the heart one believes unto righteousness, and with the mouth confession is made unto salvation***

> 2 CORINTHIANS 4:13 ***And since we have the same spirit of faith, according to what is written, "I believed and therefore I spoke," we also believe and therefore speak, And since we have the same spirit of faith, according to what is written, "I believed and therefore I spoke," we also believe and therefore speak,***

Every sinner's great need is righteousness and, to be more precise, the very righteousness of God. Nobody can generate or earn it. Instead of having the righteousness of God, the sinner practises exactly the opposite, sin. The only way to get righteousness is if it is given as a gift by God. Turning away from the old life and believing that His Son has paid the full price for salvation, gives the sinner the righteousness of God. God, using Paul, points us back to Abraham.

> ROMANS 4:3 ***For what does the Scripture say? "Abraham believed God, and it was accounted to him for righteousness."***

Believing then is absolutely essential. This is the only way to get the gift of righteousness and to escape the awful damnation of sin. The Word of God tells the sinner exactly how to receive it.

> ROMANS 10:9-10 ***... if you... believe in your heart that God has raised Him from the dead, you will be saved. For with the heart one believes unto righteousness...***

It is with the heart that one believes unto righteousness. The heart is the inner being of the person. When a sinner fully and completely believes the message of the atonement, this is believing with the heart, and this brings righteousness. God gives it as a gift when the sinner turns away from all false hopes of salvation or disbelief in God and believes that Christ made atonement for sin.

In the scripture above, Paul tells the sinner, in a brief summary, what must be believed. He says, *"If you believe with your heart that God has raised Him from the dead..."*. This is what must be believed and he elaborates in the scripture below.

> 1 CORINTHIANS 15:1-4 ***Moreover, brethren, I declare to you the gospel which I preached to you, which also you received and in which you stand, by which also you are saved, if you hold fast that word which I preached to you—unless you believed in vain. For I delivered to you first of all that which I also received: that Christ died for our sins according to the Scriptures, and that He was buried, and that He rose again the third day according to the Scriptures,***

When more and more scriptures are brought to bear on the subject, a clearer and more comprehensive statement can be developed to describe what is actually believed.

The sinner in fact believes that the perfect Son of God was born of a virgin, that He walked the earth, did not sin once, was crucified on the cross, bore the sins of the world, died a vicarious death, was buried in a tomb, was dead for three days and three nights, suffered the consequences of sin, was raised from the dead by God, is victor over sin and death, has ascended into heaven and has been exalted to the right hand of God the Father or, as Paul summarized: *"If you believe with your heart that God has raised Him from the dead..."*.

This truth must be received, embraced and whole-heartedly believed. To merely agree mentally that Jesus Christ died and rose from the dead is not sufficient. A heart believing is required. If a sinner follows the directions above, the very righteousness of God will be his or hers in a moment.

CHAPTER FIFTEEN

Confess

The next element of salvation is to confess that Jesus Christ is Lord. This is absolutely vital because believing what Christ has done in His work of atonement must be completed by an appropriate confession. The confession that is required by God is one that includes all that Christ Jesus has done in His work of atonement and all that He is.

> Romans 10:9-10 ***... if you confess with your mouth the Lord Jesus... for... with the mouth confession is made unto salvation.***

Confession that Jesus Christ is Lord has always been the central issue. People had to and still have to decide who this person, Jesus of Nazareth, really is. The Lord Jesus Christ Himself once challenged His disciples on this very issue and this incident proves how crucial this confession is.

> Matthew 16:13-17 ***When Jesus came into the region of Caesarea Philippi, He asked His disciples, saying, "Who do men say that I, the Son of Man, am?" So they said, "Some say John the Baptist, some Elijah, and others Jeremiah or one of the prophets." He said to them, "But who do you say that I am?" Simon Peter answered and said, "You are the Christ, the Son of the living God." Jesus answered and said to him, "Blessed are you, Simon Bar-Jonah, for flesh and blood has not revealed this to you, but My Father who is in heaven."***

There was great speculation and controversy as to who Jesus of Nazareth really was. Many received Him as a mere man, who had lived in the past and now reappeared on the scene. They had a strange belief that He might have been any one of many prophets such as John the Baptist, Elijah or Jeremiah, who had risen from the dead. Many believed that He was a deceiver, while others believed that He was merely a carpenter's son. The Jewish establishment considered Him just a teacher and a deceiver. The Romans considered Him as nothing but a Jewish subject.

However, the Lord asked His disciples who they believed He was. When Peter declared that He was "*the Son of the living God*", the Lord replied that Peter was blessed of God because a divine revelation had been given to him. Such a confession is required from all those who seek salvation.

The Lord Jesus Christ is no ordinary human being. He is the Son of Man and He is the Son of God. If you receive Him merely as a human being you will not be saved. He is more than that. His divinity is central to salvation.

To get the full understanding of this, one must look back at what the first believers were confessing when they said that Jesus is Lord. To confess Jesus as Lord was to them to identify Him as the Lord of the Old Testament, Who had come in the flesh. No Jew would have done this if he or she thought that He was an ordinary man or a prophet. The title Lord, in Greek, *Kurious,* was reserved only for God by the Jews. The Roman emperor Caesar demanded that he be worshipped as *Kurious,* but sincere Jews would not do so. So, when they confessed Jesus Christ as Lord, they were accepting all the claims to deity that were made by this seemingly insignificant Jew. Confessing Him as Lord was crucial to their faith.

Peter had no qualms about this. In the scripture below, he quotes from Isaiah 40:6-8 and here it is undeniably a clear reference to God.

1 PETER 1:24-25 ***For, "All people are like grass, and all their glory is like the flowers of the field; the grass withers and the flowers fall, but the word of the Lord endures forever."***

In the next chapter, he goes right ahead and uses the same title for the Lord Jesus Christ. Peter knows that Jesus Christ is uniquely the Son of God, that is God manifest in the flesh.

1 PETER 2:3 ***Now that you have tasted that the Lord is good.***

He does the same thing with another scripture that is a reference to a verse in the Book of Isaiah and equates this to Christ.

ISAIAH 8:13 ***The Lord of hosts, Him you shall hallow; Let Him be your fear, And let Him be your dread.***

1 PETER 3:15 ***but set apart Christ as Lord in your hearts (Wuest Translation)***

It is obvious that Peter was exhorting these believers to set apart the Messiah, the Lord Jesus, as Jehovah, very God, in their hearts. A Jew would never call a created being Lord. Pagan's could do that but not a Jew. To call Jesus Lord meant that they believed His claims to deity.

Going back to the days when the Lord Jesus Christ was on the earth, we see that the Lord Himself considered the title *kurious* a reference to Himself. He silenced the Pharisees when He challenged them on who the Messiah really was.

MATTHEW 22:41-46 ***While the Pharisees were gathered together, Jesus asked them, "What do you think about the Messiah? Whose son is he?" "The son of David," they replied. He said to them, "How is it then that David, speaking by the Spirit, calls him 'Lord'? For he says,"'The Lord said to my Lord: "Sit at my right hand until I put your enemies under your***

feet."' If then David calls him 'Lord,' how can he be his son?" No one could say a word in reply, and from that day on no one dared to ask him any more questions.

The Lord, in the scripture above, is clearly evoking all the Old Testament associations of Lord with Himself. The apostles and all believers did the same.

After the Lord Jesus Christ had risen from the dead, He entered a room that was securely locked, walking right through the walls. When Thomas saw this and the mortal wounds in the hands and sides of the Saviour, he immediately recognized the absolute deity of Jesus Christ and called Him *"My Lord and My God"*.

JOHN 20:27-29 ***Then he said to Thomas, "Put your finger here; see my hands. Reach out your hand and put it into my side. Stop doubting and believe." Thomas said to him, "My Lord and my God!" Then Jesus told him, "Because you have seen me, you have believed; blessed are those who have not seen and yet have believed."***

God, the Father Himself, declared that Jesus Christ was Lord, affirming that He was divine and therefore the second person of the Godhead. Jesus Christ of Nazareth is Lord.

ACTS 2:36 ***Therefore let all the house of Israel know assuredly that God has made this Jesus, whom you crucified, both Lord and Christ."***

ACTS 10:36 ***The word which God sent to the children of Israel, preaching peace through Jesus Christ—He is Lord of all***

In order for a sinner to complete the third element of salvation, he or she must acknowledge who Christ is and must also confess Him as Lord. If the sinners consider Him to be merely a prophet or a teacher or just a good example they will fall far short of the confession that is required of them.

Jesus Christ is the eternal Son of God. He is the second person of the Godhead, who appeared in the flesh. Nobody can get around that. To confess Him as anything less, is to deny the clear teachings of scripture.

> 1 TIMOTHY 3:16 ***And without controversy great is the mystery of godliness: God was manifested in the flesh, justified in the Spirit, seen by angels, preached among the Gentiles, believed on in the world, received up in glory.***

In the days of the Gospels and in the Book of Acts, sinners became believers when they confessed Christ publicly. They did this in the face of disapproval and later on directly in the face of threats of death. When faced with death, true believers refused to back down, but held fast to their confession that Jesus Christ was Lord.

A sinner's confession must also be a public one. Praying the sinner's prayer in private and never coming out and telling others will result in a faith unborn. Many want to be saved but will not confess Christ as Lord because they fear human disapproval. However, when it is realized that such a confession is waited for in heaven, they become emboldened to do so.

> MATTHEW 10:32 ***Therefore whoever confesses Me before men, him I will also confess before My Father who is in heaven. But whoever denies Me before men, him I will also deny before My Father who is in heaven***

One must remember that one's confession that Jesus Christ is Lord is directly connected to heaven. The Lord is in heaven and at the right hand of the Father. He waits for the sinner to repent, to believe and to confess Him as Lord. When he or she does that in all sincerity, He steps in on their behalf and the Father then releases eternal life into your spirit.

> HEBREWS 3:1 ***Therefore, holy brethren, partakers of the heavenly calling, consider the Apostle and High Priest of our confession, Christ Jesus***

Everybody will eventually confess that Jesus Christ is Lord. Some will do it this side of the grave, and that will result in their salvation, and other's will finally admit that He is Lord on Judgment Day, and that to their own regret.

> PHILIPPIANS 2:9-11 ***Therefore God also has highly exalted Him and given Him the name which is above every name, that at the name of Jesus every knee should bow, of those in heaven, and of those on earth, and of those under the earth, and that every tongue should confess that Jesus Christ is Lord, to the glory of God the Father.***

Why should a sinner wait until he or she dies before admitting that Jesus is Lord and then perish in his or her sins? It would be much better to confess Jesus Christ as Lord this side of the grave.

CHAPTER SIXTEEN

Corresponding Faith Actions

THE FOURTH ELEMENT OF SALVATION is *Corresponding Faith Actions.* The sinner must first turn away from all false hopes of salvation or a disregard of God, believe what Christ has done for him or her and then confess that Jesus Christ is Lord. This produces faith. However, faith by itself is dead. Corresponding faith actions must follow. This gives life to the faith that is in the heart of the new believer. Faith must work together with corresponding faith actions for it to be made perfect.

JAMES 2:22 ***Do you see that faith was working together with his works, and by works faith was made perfect?***

The *"works"* in the scripture above and below do not refer to good works, such as feeding and clothing the poor, but refer to corresponding faith actions. Corresponding faith actions are the outward demonstrations of the heart faith that is being confessed. This gives credence to the confession.

JAMES 2:17 ***Thus also faith by itself, if it does not have works, is dead.***

Faith is like a human body. Without the spirit, a body is dead. People bury such a body. The spirit of the faith that believes in Christ, is the action that lines up and accompanies the confession.

> James 2:26 ***...for as the body without the spirit is dead, so faith without works is dead also.***

Below are some of the *Corresponding Faith Actions* that give life to the faith that the new believer possesses and he or she is responsible for the production of these.

Once the new believer has received faith in his or her heart, it must be expressed in action. One way that it is expressed is when the irrepressible desire to thank God for His wonderful gift of salvation is released in thanksgiving. The new believer's breaking forth into thanksgiving and praise is *faith works.* This is essential. Faith speaks. Faith cannot help but speak and tell others of the wonderful free grace of God.

> 2 Corinthians 4:13 ***We having the same spirit of faith, according as it is written, I believed, and therefore have I spoken; we also believe, and therefore speak***

Faith is like a fountain in the new believer's heart. It must be released. If a person has received *the faith that saves* in his or her heart, then it will seek expression because faith without works is dead.

When a new believer receives faith, he or she cannot help but rush to join a body of believers. This does not get the person saved but the action releases the dynamic faith that is resident in the heart and brings it out into the open. If this action is not there, then the faith dies. This corresponding faith action must follow because it brings to life what is believed in the heart and confessed with the mouth. If a person says that he or she repents, believes and confesses that Jesus Christ is Lord but never joins the fellowship of the believers, one wonders what the sinner's prayer was all about. This kind of faith is dead and is ready to be buried.

Once people get saved and join a fellowship of believers, more corresponding faith actions will follow. There they will pray. There they will worship God. There they might serve as ushers. There they might serve as musicians. There they will give. There they will involve themselves in various ministries. There they will preach the gospel. These are corresponding faith actions of new believers that line up with the claim that salvation has been received.

After getting saved a corresponding faith action would be a submission to water baptism, which is in itself a confession of faith and of the Lordship of Jesus Christ. Seeking and receiving the baptism in the Holy Spirit is also proof of a heart faith in the resurrection of the Lord.

Corresponding faith actions are easily recognizable in the lives of the new believers. They start working at getting out of sin. Those who are bound in smoking and drinking, break off from those things. Nobody has to tell someone who is saved to stop going to nightclubs or to wild parties. They just stop going and find no delight in those things. If they are living in adultery, they come under conviction and break off these relationships or get married. A saved person comes under great conviction if they lie or steal and they always work to get this out of their lives. Those who are saved, depart from iniquity. These are the *works* that express faith.

Corresponding Faith Actions give spirit to the faith that the new believer has in his or her heart. These kind of works, when expressed in the lives of new believers, perfects, gives substance and drives the new believer's faith.

CHAPTER SEVENTEEN

Evidence of Salvation

IF THE SINNER HAS ACTED upon the Word of God, as described earlier, that person will be saved and the proof of it is simply the fact that they have acted upon the Word of God. That settles the matter. However, there are other evidences of salvation for everyone to see if a sinner has genuinely and sincerely acted on God's Word, and been saved. Other believers will readily acknowledge the new believer's salvation as genuine if these things are evident in their lives.

The first evidence of salvation is the fact that the person will have a *full assurance of salvation*. All new believers have the *"I know that I know, that I know, that I know, that I know,... that I am saved,"* knowledge in them. This will always be very evident in a new believer. When this is expressed in corresponding faith actions, other believers will be convinced that the person is saved. This knowledge is granted to them by God Himself. All believers have the witness in them and can't help but know that their salvation is real.

> ROMANS 8:16 ***The Spirit Himself bears witness with our spirit that we are children of God***

A new believer will look no further. The believer has found the *Pearl of Great Price* and has no reason to look for another. Searching ends when Jesus Christ is found. The next quest is simply to grow in fellowship with the Lord, with the Father and in the sweet communion of the Holy Spirit.

MATTHEW 13:45-46 ***Again, the kingdom of heaven is like a merchant seeking beautiful pearls, who, when he had found one pearl of great price, went and sold all that he had and bought it.***

A unique sign in new believers is their bold confession that Jesus Christ is Lord. A sinner cannot do this, but a believer can. When sinners get saved, they are not ashamed of the name of Jesus Christ anymore and no longer refer to Him as "*the big man up there*". Those who have previously denied Christ or have been embarrassed to mention His name, suddenly boldly do so.

ROMANS 1:16 ***For I am not ashamed of the gospel of Christ, for it is the power of God to salvation for everyone who believes, for the Jew first and also for the Greek.***

A saved person comes under conviction. If he or she was afraid to mention that Jesus Christ is their Lord, just because of the fear of the faces of men, this changes. He is Lord and they become willing to die for Him. New believers share their new found faith with enthusiasm and are amazed that other people cannot see the reality of salvation.

MATTHEW 10:32-33 ***Therefore whoever confesses Me before men, him I will also confess before My Father who is in heaven. But whoever denies Me before men, him I will also deny before My Father who is in heaven.***

Evidence that a new believer has entered into salvation is the fact that, without being told to do so, they break off their old religious affiliations and join themselves to other believers. What the first believers did on the day of Pentecost, all believers do in this present day.

ACTS 2:40-47 ***... Then those who gladly received his word were baptized; and that day about three thousand souls were added to them.***

When a new believer joins the assembly of believers, those who are saved recognize that the person is now saved. Only a saved person will enter into joyful praising and worshipping of God and will seek out fellowship with other saved people.

Those who are saved do not hold fast to their old sins but turn away from such wholeheartedly. People who openly practise sin as a lifestyle cannot be saved.

> 2 TIMOTHY 2:19 ***Nevertheless the solid foundation of God stands, having this seal: "The Lord knows those who are His," and, "Let everyone who names the name of Christ depart from iniquity."***

They don't only depart from sin but cannot live the lifestyle of sin.

> 1 JOHN 3:6 ***Whoever abides in Him does not sin. Whoever sins has neither seen Him nor known Him.***

A saved person has the attitude spoken of in the scripture below. They do not seek mercy for salvation because they have been cleansed from their old sins. However, because they are saved and know that they are, they know that they must not cover their sins but should confess and forsake them. It is wonderful to see new believers kicking at and punching at sin.

> PROVERBS 28:13 ***He who covers his sins will not prosper, But whoever confesses and forsakes them will have mercy.***

New believers who have increased their goods by robbing others before salvation are convicted and seek ways to make amends. Others who have done wrong to people in the recent past go and ask forgiveness. New believers try to fix the wrongs of the past, as far as they can.

EXODUS 22:5 ***If a man causes a field or vineyard to be grazed, and lets loose his animal, and it feeds in another man's field, he shall make restitution from the best of his own field and the best of his own vineyard.***

Sure evidence that a person is saved is that they begin to serve the Lord. They throw themselves wholeheartedly into the work of God.

1 THESSALONIANS 1:9 ***For they themselves declare concerning us what manner of entry we had to you, and how you turned to God from idols to serve the living and true God,***

The Lord knows those who are His and those who are not His. Believers, in all sincerity, refer to Him as Lord. They enter into fellowship with the Father and the Father with them. They start to get into communion with the Holy Spirit and the Holy Spirit with them.

CHAPTER EIGHTEEN

Continuing

Continuing is a word that I use to describe the keeping of oneself in, holding fast and persevering in the vital mode of faith that was entered into at the time when salvation was received. Although *Continuing* does not give salvation, it drives, maintains and keeps the faith alive.

After the sinner gets saved, he or she must continue in the faith. The person must not start out in faith and then end up in unbelief. The Word of God is clear on the issue. One cannot continue in faith for a while and then abandon it and return to the old natural life. "Once saved, always saved" is a false teaching. Paul, writing to the Corinthians, makes this clear.

> 1 Corinthians 15:1-2 ***Moreover, brethren, I declare to you the gospel which I preached to you, which also you received and in which you stand, by which also you are saved, if you hold fast that word which I preached to you—unless you believed in vain.***

Notice that Paul says that they *are saved* and that they *stand* in the gospel, but that they remain in salvation if they, *"hold fast that word"*. Paul was direct, instructing them that they would not be in right-standing with God if the initial works of faith were abandoned. It is clear, then, that all believers remain in the blessed space of salvation if they hold fast to their faith. He seals this important and absolutely crucial element of salvation with the words, *"unless you believed in vain"*. Any believer can decide to depart from the faith. Paul, John and James also taught along the same vein throughout their epistles.

1 CORINTHIANS 16:13 ***Watch, stand fast in the faith, be brave, be strong. Let all that you do be done with love.***

It stands to reason that if a believer is told to *stand fast in the faith,* that must mean that the person could turn back. The believer has received salvation as a gift but must stand his or her ground, in faith, in the face of every challenge.

2 CORINTHIANS 1:24 ***Not that we have dominion over your faith, but are fellow workers for your joy; for by faith you stand.***

The scripture is self-explanatory. It is by faith that the believer stands. The new believer must therefore stand in faith and do everything to stand in faith and when that is done he or she must continue to stand, in faith.

In the daily life of the Christian there are many things that happen. Sometimes they get caught up in un-forgiveness and bitterness and get themselves all tangled up in things that do not line up with holiness. Eventually they get to a place where they seem to live the same lifestyle as the sinner. Paul says that they could be disqualified, so they should examine themselves to see whether they are in faith. They should test themselves to make sure that they are continuing in the faith. There is always the danger of turning back to unbelief.

2 CORINTHIANS 13:5 ***Examine yourselves as to whether you are in the faith. Test yourselves. Do you not know yourselves, that Jesus Christ is in you?—unless indeed you are disqualified.***

The child of God must continue in the faith. How much clearer can it be set forth before the eyes of the believer?

COLOSSIANS 1:23 ***if indeed you continue in the faith, grounded and steadfast, and are not moved away from the hope of the gospel which you***

heard, which was preached to every creature under heaven, of which I, Paul, became a minister.

The whole argument of the letter to the Hebrews is that the believers spoken of there should not turn back from faith in Christ. If they did that, they would lose what they had received from God. Paul tries to convince the turning back Hebrews to go on in faith and pleads with them to hold fast to the confidence that they had in Christ Jesus the Lord.

HEBREWS 10:35 ***Therefore do not cast away your confidence, which has great reward.***

Believers are not only in danger of gradually falling back into unbelief and sin; they can actually come to a place when they can reject the Lord Jesus Christ and sin a sin that leads to the second death.

1 JOHN 5:16 ***If anyone sees his brother sinning a sin which does not lead to death, he will ask, and He will give him life for those who commit sin not leading to death. There is sin leading to death. I do not say that he should pray about that.***

Even mature Christians can *fall away*. The scripture below needs much comment but just a cursory reading of the scripture below proves this to be true.

HEBREWS 6:4-6 ***For it is impossible for those who were once enlightened, and have tasted the heavenly gift, and have become partakers of the Holy Spirit, and have tasted the good word of God and the powers of the age to come, if they fall away, to renew them again to repentance, since they crucify again for themselves the Son of God, and put Him to an open shame.***

All believers, in order to make sure that they are continuing in the Lord, must make their call and election sure. Peter exhorts the believer in this direction.

> 2 PETER 1:10 ***Therefore, brethren, be even more diligent to make your call and election sure, for if you do these things you will never stumble;***

Notice the words, *"you will never stumble"*. Making the calling and election sure anchors the believer in the faith that has brought him or her salvation. This is not a works programme that is necessary after salvation but is rather a developing of the fruits of the spirit in the life of the believer. Peter gives a list to work on.

> 2 PETER 1:5-11 ***But also for this very reason, giving all diligence, add to your faith virtue, to virtue knowledge, to knowledge self-control, to self-control perseverance, to perseverance godliness, to godliness brotherly kindness, and to brotherly kindness love. For if these things are yours and abound, you will be neither barren nor unfruitful in the knowledge of our Lord Jesus Christ. For he who lacks these things is short sighted, even to blindness, and has forgotten that he was cleansed from his old sins. Therefore, brethren, be even more diligent to make your call and election sure, for if you do these things you will never stumble; for so an entrance will be supplied to you abundantly into the everlasting kingdom of our Lord and Saviour Jesus Christ.***

As these wonderful graces get developed in the believer's life, the world, and the lifestyle that goes with it, is pushed into the distant past.

The believer must continue in the Lord, be steadfast, immovable, holding fast to the word that got him or her saved. Believers must grow in grace and in the knowledge of Christ Jesus their saviour, and make their calling and election sure and they will be safe.

The Sinner's Prayer

Every sinner who is convinced by the Word of God and wants to be saved should pray the prayer given below.

Almighty God, I am a sinner. I have continually violated Your righteousness by refusing to submit to your eternal rule. Hell is my final destination, if I should die in my sins. I have not only rejected your righteous rule but, in my pursuit of sin, I have neglected the free gift of salvation. I have, I realize now, with grief, dishonoured the great King of heaven and earth. My only hope is if You extend mercy to me now. If not, I will perish in the eternal sufferings of the Lake of Fire.

Almighty God, I now turn away from my rebellion. Today and right now I turn away from every false hope of salvation, disbelief and of disregarding You. You have directed sinners to repent and to accept the free gift of salvation that you have provided through Jesus Christ, the Son of God. Please forgive me as I do so now.

I do believe that the Lord Jesus Christ died for me on the cross, suffered for me and has fully paid the price for sin. I embrace this truth with all my heart. I also confess with my own mouth that Jesus Christ is Lord. He is the Son of God.

I now lift up my hands to You, Almighty God, and utter my first hallelujah! Hallelujah!

Your Word is true, so I know that You have forgiven me and washed away my sins. I can therefore boldly declare that I am saved. Thank You for saving me.

I sign my name here as an act of faith, declaring that Jesus Christ, the Lord of Lords, is my eternal saviour.

Name:..

Author's Final Word

Everyone should read this book. If you are not saved, follow the clear path to salvation and don't stop until you are safely in the Kingdom of God.

After you are saved, hold onto this book. I recommend you keep it with your bible. Read it many times and underline that which becomes revelation to you. Continue to study the book until you are very familiar with the doctrine of salvation. The knowledge will be extremely useful to you in the future.

This book is an excellent soul-winning tool. It can be used by those who are zealous to win the lost for Christ. Use the knowledge in the book to give witness to the lost. It is best to give the sinner a copy and to work through the book with him or her until the person takes the necessary steps to salvation.

Whenever possible, place this book in the hand of a prisoner, someone who is in hospital or bedridden at home. Give this book as a gift to unsaved family members, friends, neighbours and work colleagues or to strangers whom you wish to lead to Christ.

Preachers and teachers can extract topics to preach on or to teach. Messages can be preached and taught on Divine Government, The Soul who Sins shall die, The Guilt of the Sinner, The Atonement, False Hopes of the Sinner, Disregard for God, The Sinner's Salvation, Evidence of Salvation, Continuing in the Lord and many more.

This book is part of a series of books that are perfect for a Foundational Principles Class. They can be taught over three months, over six months and even over a year. Pastors will find these books very helpful in church work. If these truths are inculcated in the hearers, they will be rapidly transformed into Word-based believers.

www.ingramcontent.com/pod-product-compliance
Lightning Source LLC
Chambersburg PA
CBHW021210020426
42331CB00003B/287

* 9 7 8 0 6 2 0 7 8 2 6 5 4 *